The Option Method Joybuilding Workbook

The Option Method Joybuilding Workbook

Frank Mosca Ph.D.

Writers Club Press

San Jose   New York   Lincoln   Shanghai

The Option Method Joybuilding Workbook

All Rights Reserved © 2002 by Frank Mosca

No part of this book may be reproduced or transmitted in any form or by any means, graphic, electronic, or mechanical, including photocopying, recording, taping, or by any information storage retrieval system, without the permission in writing from the publisher.

Writers Club Press
an imprint of iUniverse, Inc.

For information address:
iUniverse, Inc.
5220 S. 16th St., Suite 200
Lincoln, NE 68512
www.iuniverse.com

Cartoon characters courtesy of Microsoft Clipart®

This approach is not meant to diagnose or treat any entity called a mental illness. Please consult a professional if you feel you need that kind of assistance.

ISBN: 0-595-21774-5

Printed in the United States of America

Dedication

To all those who helped me on the road to happiness: parents, brother, wife, Linda, children, friends, Guy, Option Method Group classmates, Debbie, Mandy, Bears, Roedi and of course Bruce. Gratitude forever.

Contents

List of Illustrations

Preface

The "Magic" Ball: a tale of two perspectives by Frank Mosca

Once there were two children Tommy and Teddy who were best friends and inseparable playmates. They lived in the country and had plenty of wonderful open green fields to run and frolic in and be together especially in the lazy, languid, long days of summer. As they were playing one day they came upon a strange sight. In a small glen near their homes they found two identical red balls about five inches in diameter lying on the ground one right next to the other. They ran up to them and without a word each one grabbed a ball and began to play with it. Since there were two identical balls, there was absolutely no problem initially. It seemed clear they both had started with exactly the same object, with the same characteristics of weight, buoyancy, elasticity and texture.

So they played side by side, each with his own ball for a while. As time passed, however, it became apparent that some difference in their experience of playing with the red balls was emerging. Tommy was consistently so much more engaged with his ball. He relished all of its potentials. He felt greater glee and abandon as he threw it up as high as he could. Whether he actually caught it or whether he missed it and it bounced on the ground and he had to run and retrieve it, he was equally satisfied. He loved its feel, he loved the way it hit the ground with sometimes a soft thud on the grass or a sharper springy sound on harder bare spots or still a different sound on rocks. He relished the different, unpredictable paths it would take when he missed it and it went off bounding against trees and making a zig zag path through a bed of flowers. Even the smell of the ball, how it felt against his face: all these seemingly endless dimensions played on his senses like an accomplished musician on a grand piano and he would constantly let out peals of laughter and squeals of delight.

Teddy, however, was having a different experience. He became increasingly frustrated when he failed to catch the ball. He found it awkward and uninteresting when he had to chase it and retrieve it from some crack or crevice it might lodge itself in or when he had to search for a while because it was hiding in a bush or thicket. He wanted the ball to react differently. It seemed too light; its feel for him was that he could not adequately find a comfortable grip to accomplish what he wanted to accomplish with it. The growing dissatisfaction seemed to interfere with his ability to gain altitude when he threw it up in the air because he was concentrating so hard on trying to put a certain kind of spin on it, that the effort became too complicated and in the end he simply dropped the ball and let it roll away from him, sat down and watched Tommy play. Tommy seemed so totally absorbed in his joy with the ball, the ball seemed to act so much differently in his hands, that Teddy gradually came to the conclusion that however identical the balls seemed when they were lying together upon first finding them, they quite clearly were not the same. Tommy had somehow gotten the better ball, the "magic" ball, with better handling characteristics and Teddy settled into a jealous funk as he continued to see how much enjoyment Tommy continued to have with his ball. Finally, unable to contain himself he ran up to Tommy and kicked the ball away out of his hands as it returned to earth from a particularly high arc that Tommy had achieved with it. "Darn," said Teddy, "you got the better ball, Tommy, and that's simply not fair. I have spent the last 20 minutes playing with my ball and it doesn't do half the things that you are doing with yours. The least you can do, if you are really my friend, is let me have your red ball so that I can have the same kind of fun you are having."

Tommy stopped in his tracks, watched his own red ball trail off into a small gully where Teddy had kicked it, and looked back directly at him. "Okay Teddy," he said with a smile, "you can play with it. That's fine with me." He even went over and retrieved it and handed it to Teddy. "Please, take it and enjoy yourself. With your permission, I will play with your red ball." Teddy nodded enthusiastically and Tommy went off to retrieve that ball. Meanwhile Teddy fondled the "magic good ball" and began putting it through its paces in full expectation and anticipation of having as good a time as Tommy since now, he thought, he clearly had a ball that was capable of providing him with a good time. He tried the tricks he wished to make happen with the new ball. But, try as he might, the ball seemed some how to change in his hands. It had the same characteristics as the other ball, the "bad" ball, with the same obvious defects and shortcomings in its structure and potentials. How could that be? Meanwhile Tommy had retrieved the "bad" red ball and had resumed play with it. Lo and behold, he was having the same good time and the same wonderful results that he had with the "magic" ball that Teddy now held in his hands. Teddy now became angry and resentful, dropped the "magic" ball and confronted Tommy with his suspicions about the balls. Tommy was puzzled but listened to his friend respectfully. He offered to change balls again. Teddy was not satisfied. "You must be doing something to the balls to make such a difference," Teddy shouted and he started to cry. Tommy approached him and put a hand on his shoulder. "I don't know what to say, Teddy," he said, "I don't experience any difference and I sure don't know how to change anything about those two red balls. I am just so happy and pleased to have discovered them and see what they can do." "But then why won't the balls do what I want them to do?" replied Teddy, softening in response to Tommy's kind touch, "I would love to have fun with them like you, but they just won't behave in a way that I can enjoy, so I am really disappointed that we ever found them Tommy." "Well I really don't know why that is, but maybe, Teddy, if you didn't have so many rules about how that ball had to act for you, you would be a lot happier with what that red ball could be for you just the way that it is?"

"Yeah, but I believe a ball should do certain things and for me, if it doesn't do that, then I don't think it's a good ball at all," said Teddy emphatically. "That's sure a way you can think about that, Teddy, but for me I'm happy just seeing what the ball can do for itself. Why don't you give it a chance to show you?" Teddy was sullen and resistant at first, but then, he got up, took hold of the red ball he originally started with and began to pay attention to some of the things that had so engaged Tommy, the texture, its sense of roundness, its rubbery smell mixed now with faint scents of grass, weeds and flowers. He just dropped it and let it roll however it would. He allowed himself to be delighted by the paths it would take and the places it would discover for him. At one point he discovered this really neat turtle sitting in the cleft of a rock where the ball had rolled and he called Tommy over excitedly. They both laughed for minutes on end as the turtle nuzzled the ball with its beak and sent it off rolling in another direction. Gosh, they had met another friend in this meadow, a friend introduced to them by what Teddy now considered definitely to be *the* "magic" ball. The day progressed and gradually Teddy began to get into the same flow of joy and abandon that Tommy had allowed to delight him earlier in the day. Finally, it was time to leave and they came to the fork in the road where they would head for their respective homes. They paused, gave each other a friendly shove and Teddy sheepishly held out his red ball to Tommy saying, "hey Tommy, I had great fun with this one. Would you like to take it, 'cause I think this one is the *real* "magic" ball?" Tommy giggled delightedly while shaking his head "no" and said: "Gee, Teddy, I think the magic is more in this ball, than in any "magic" ball," and he accompanied his words by rubbing his hand roughly but lovingly through Teddy's hair and then ever so softly touching Teddy's chest. "That's the magic ball; you've got yours and I've got mine," he said as he pointed to his own head and then his own heart. "Hey, see ya tomorrow, and don't forget to bring your magic ball," he shouted back over his shoulder with a laugh as he picked up his pace and began to run home.

Introduction

THE TRUTH: Therefore, the beginning point, the Great Truth we start with, is that we know that people believe that unhappiness is necessary, and that is why they are unhappy. It is almost beside the point to believe that people get unhappy, or make themselves unhappy….They believe they must be unhappy, and are suffering because they believe it is an inescapable truth. Unhappiness is simply believing; not being, or getting, or making or doing unhappiness.

The Founder of Option, Bruce Di Marsico

INTRODUCTION TO THE JOYBUILDING SYSTEM WORKBOOK

Greetings. Congratulations on the purchase of this Joybuilding system. Let me begin by what may seem a startling statement. You do not need this book or my other published materials, or anybody else's for that matter, in order to be happy! Now if this prompts you to run to the post office or the book store and return the whole package, wait just one minute while I explain. Your happiness is not the result of anything I have written or said. Your happiness is your birthright; it belongs to you alone and cannot be purchased or created at the hands of someone other than you. What I claim is that the Option Method is the second best way of realizing your happiness; the first is you simply being happy without any guidelines or exercises or any other fussing of any kind.

However, you may have acquired this package precisely because you do not yet possess the comprehension of that intimate personal joyous truth. Ah, then, my friend, you are in for a treat, because everything that follows is designed to aid you in opening up those personal doors to the truth about your own happiness.

HOW TO USE THIS JOY BUILDING SYSTEM WORKBOOK

This book is designed to help you organize your thoughts so as to optimize your understanding of the Option Method and its potential to aid you in recognizing and affirming the truth about your happiness. That is what I call your **JOYWORK.** After a brief introduction, the Option Method questions will be presented along with the "ABC's" of understanding both happiness and unhappiness. Every attempt will be made to keep you fully informed and take you step by step through your Joywork. The questions are the heart of the Method, and a deep acquaintance with, meditation on, and active use of them is the key to the success of your Joywork. You will find other components of the Joybuilding System (the books, *Joywords, The Unbearable Wrongness of Being,* the novel, *The God-Speak* and other materials, i.e., audio or video tapes, as they become available) to be of particular help in giving you both written and live action examples of how the Method is applied to real people, just like you. Please remember also that you can find timely updates about my work and what might be available to enhance your joywork on my website *http://frankmosca.com* at any time. The idea is to work intensively with the Method and use this workbook to record your responses. The workbook can stand on its own, but with the other components added, you simply increase your resources for building your joy. That's okay with you, right? So, mark this book up like crazy. Also, use a notebook, keep a journal, make the material your own. This is after all your happiness we are talking about, not anyone else's.

We will start with a bit about me, then look at the ABC's of happiness and unhappiness. After the Option Method questions themselves will come a section that will address key concepts so as to give you a thorough education in what is behind the Option Method. These concepts will be followed by two major sections, one on Unhappiness and the other on Happiness. Major categories of unhappiness will be explored and explained from the Option perspective and then questions will be given to provoke some useful exploration. Additionally, each category will have a set of experiential exercises, exper/cises for short, that will hopefully allow you to recognize and release the beliefs that are your unhappiness. Okay? Then one final note before we get started.

The questions and exercises you will encounter in the Workbook are meant to be a guide and inspiration to evoke your own inquisitive faculties, to provoke a journey fashioned by you alone into the endless wealth of your own joy and happiness. What they do not represent is a new way that you "have to be" in order to be happy! This is not a kind of "bible" that you are to read and memorize and make reference to in a blind faith way. No, everything that will be presented to you will be totally and completely based on *experiential truth*. The explanations involve intellectual reason and understanding, but the truth is that you will either feel/experience the truth about your happiness or you will not. When you *do* then you will immediately understand that all the words, explanations, images were there for only one reason: *to aid you in experiencing that truth of your joy.*

Indeed, when you come to utilize this workbook, as I hope you will, as a treasure beyond counting to remind you of your happiness and as a tool to deepen your joy and elation, it will not be because of the magic of my words, but because my words have become the occasion for you to create your own language of happiness. You will record your experiences, meditations, images and enlightenment over time. This will be the monument to the love you bear yourself; this will be the heart of your own personal gospel. It will not be revealed by some other agency, but created by your own joyous discoveries and expanded, I hope, each and every day by a continuous exploration and awakening to the boundless potentials of what it is like to be you and live the truth of your happiness.

What the Option Method is about is realizing your happiness. It is not about trying to be "authentic" or "spiritually advanced" or part of an elevated "selfhood" open only to the special initiates of some arcane process. Many disciplines strive for authenticity, spiritual advancement or enlightenment. Yet, what they really are searching for is their happiness. Option cuts to the core of what we truly want: our happiness and joy. There is no greater truth than your happiness. And what I call the "Great Democracy of Being" gives all equal access to that truth about themselves because the access resides with them and not with some other agent or authority. What these explanations and exper/cises are meant to be are suggested pathways, not the precepts of a new, rigid orthodoxy of happiness. Again, only your actual experience of success in utilizing this approach will validate any of the statements in this Workbook.

Let me also note that you will find a good deal of repetition of basic concepts as you go along. That is because the fundamental thesis of this work, that you don't have to be unhappy, you merely believe you do, is so radical and far reaching. I consider it important, therefore to make sure that this message is repeated dozens of times, in different contexts to be sure, but nonetheless, repeated so that it will have a chance to compete with some of the undoubtedly strong assumptions about happiness and unhappiness that you bring to the reading of this work.

This Joybuilding System Workbook is as powerful as your openness to the message of Option. That message is one that humans have awaited from the dawn of true self-reflective consciousness. Over scores of generations back into the misty beginnings of human existence, it has eluded the most enlightened souls, however they may have hovered near the truth that Option represents:

HAPPINESS IS! It is You! All have a right to their own being, that is to say, to be happy. Yes I know, this is a bold statement and no one would expect you to have an experiential sense of that just starting out in your Joywork.

UNHAPPINESS IS NOT! It is merely a belief. It has no substance, identity, reality outside the mere belief that it is. What you feel is the belief, not some objective entity called unhappiness. No matter what form your unhappiness takes, it is never anything more than a belief, i.e., you believing in whatever it is that is manifesting as the feeling you are feeling i.e., sadness, grief, anger, guilt, loneliness, etc. This too will be explored fully as we go along.

That is the Truth of Option. To know this is to be liberated forever from the illusory specter of unhappiness. It is your birthright NOW. Hopefully if you have not been living that truth as fully as you would wish, after doing your Joywork with this Option Method Joybuilding System, you will consider surrendering any final shreds of reserve about doing so.

THE METHOD

The most direct method for living your happiness is simply to live it. You don't need me, as I said initially, or your Aunt Rose or your Uncle Harry. Not at all. No questions or queries of any kind are required except the direct experience of actually being happy. However, since that is not the experience most humans report having, then there is the Option Method to help demythologize the apparent tangle of unhappiness and release us into our true state of joy. So that's where I come in.

THE QUESTIONS

The questions are designed to lay bare the shadowy, ultimately phantom nature of unhappiness. The complexities and labyrinthine anatomy of all unhappiness is mere appearance, like a ball of string that looks hopelessly knotted into a million loops and twirls all disappearing into one another; yet a tug on the end of the string reveals that it is all a crowd of phony tangles that straighten out immediately when pulled with the truth into the simplicity of a single string.

CHAPTER ONE

HAPPINESS BY THE NUMBERS AND THE ABC'S OF BLISS AND THE BLUES

Let's begin with "Happiness by the Numbers," a section of 12 titles. We'll start with some brief, simple personal observations and then expand into an explanation and overview of the three questions that are at the heart of the Option Method for Joybuilding. Then we will explore a menu of basic themes that will give you an education in the basis for the worldview that flows from an understanding of the ABC's and the Option Method.

1. You do want your happiness, don't you? You do want your joy when you experience the touch of your lover's skin, the feel of sand slightly wet with summer sea water, the thrill of throwing a ball as far as you can, the whole body feel of the wind pushing against you with your arms outstretched, your eyes closed and the smell of fresh cut grass filling your nose and lungs.

You do want all of that and more, much more. Do you have it? Do you have it *now*? Take a journey with me. My name is Frank Mosca and I am the author of this Joybuilding Workbook. Together we are going to look at the things you want, the things that stand in the way of what you want, and how you might get more of the things you want by getting rid of the things that stand in the way. Is that agreeable with you? If so, let's move on.

2. I have searched all my life for my joy. Oh, it was there from time to time, but not in any reliable way. Part of the scheme I came up with was that to be joyful, I had to be smart. I had to understand things. There must be some really complex, difficult puzzle to figure out, I thought. So I looked at really complex difficult puzzles. They were there. Plenty of them and there were also thinkers and gurus always telling me what was wrong with me, what was wrong with the way I ate, the way I made love, the way I dealt with myself, the way I dealt with others. They were sometimes partially correct, at least as I see it now. Then there were those who said that my problems were deep within me, hidden from me and only by some expert's analysis could I dig them out of the hard rock of my unconscious self. Hey, I even became one of those experts. What better way to figure yourself out than by becoming one of the people that people come to, to figure themselves out? Well, I hope that I did no more harm than most well meaning folks who try to figure themselves out by figuring other people out.

So okay, that did not do the trick, for me at least. Then I came upon something so simple, so outrageously unthinkable as to strike my polished, professional, philosophical mind as ridiculous. My joy, my happiness was always mine to have. I just didn't believe that it was. Wait a minute, I said. What would happen to my sense of the tragic in life, what would I do with my existential angst? Where would I get the great wisdom from the pains and agonies of depression and despair? It took four years of college, eight years of graduate school, not to mention years in a psychotherapy institute and other training that cost a zillion bucks to get me "smart". Didn't help. So, how did I get from smart to happy? I found someone who had discovered this simple truth, was living it, and was offering a way for others to understand it for themselves. His name was Bruce Di Marsico and he died in December of 1995.

Now, did I become instantly happy, instantly joyful and remain that way? No, that is not what happened. But what did happen was I discovered that I COULD BE instantly happy, instantly joyful. I just had to want this and work at living it in each moment. Come on now! You don't want to work? I asked you in the opening lines of this book, "Do you want your happiness?" You did say yes, didn't you? Of course you did, so let's look at the work involved for what it really is. Joywork. That's what it is. I will be along each step of the way, but it will be your Joywork we are talking about.

So we have established that, one, you want your happiness. And two, you are willing to work for it. Now we are ready to go on to the next number and find out how best to do that Joywork.

3. When my friend and late mentor Bruce came upon the understanding that he could live his joy each moment, he put it in the language that you find in the first quote on the first page of this book. What stands in the way of our being happy is our **belief** that it is *impossible not to be unhappy.* That's how it looks, right? Okay, that is certainly how it feels to us. We are not going to challenge every moment of unhappiness that you have right now. First let us learn the anatomy of unhappiness and then let's look at what can be done about it.

Try this on for size: the truth about you and the world/ the **"ABC's" of happiness and unhappiness:**

A/ There is just you and the world (includes all other people and things)
B/ You don't control the world. (The attempt to control the world has been the focus of much of human history and all of human technology.

Despite advances, our control is tenuous at best. This is actually as we will see, the main source of dread and unhappiness.)
C/ You do control the attitude that you construct toward whatever the world presents to you each moment of your existence.

Now how about it? I bet you accept A and B (though you sure do try to have as much control of the world as you can), but have trouble with C. Right?

Well it is right there in "C" that the problem arises. If "C" is not true then the ball game is over as it pertains to your ability to live your joy each moment. Might as well pack up your bags and move back in with your parents, because someone else is calling the shots on your ability to experience happiness. So if A is true and C is not true then B is the arena where you have to try to find your happiness. That would require you to control the world and all the consequences and outcomes in the world in order for your happiness and joy to be assured. Not too likely.

Which brings us to C: while it may not seem true right now, you may come to a different conclusion as you do your Joywork. That's what this whole book and your Joywork is helping you to change your mind about. Yes, I know unhappiness in whatever form just seems to rise up in response to the world. Well, if it didn't feel natural to feel unhappy, then who would ever bother to feel it? Would you? How to explain this? Belief. Yes, that's right, belief. Just as I mentioned a moment ago. That's how I will explain it to you.

Unhappiness depends on beliefs for its "charge." In order for there to be unhappiness, you have to put in your two cents worth of evaluation. It's called *meaning* or *value*. If something doesn't have meaning or value for you then your response to it is going to be close to zero. Just imagine you are doing your morning jog or walk and you pass old Mrs. Thistlewood's house, you know the one on the corner that always looks like the porch is going to collapse. You know how she likes to chew your ear and you always pray she won't be out when you pass, but there she is waiting in the road, breathless with the news of the latest tragedy to befall her. It seems that her pet worm, Freddy, has been devoured by some nasty little sparrow. You stop. You put on a face of commiseration. But, are you really going to be broken up over poor Freddy's demise? I don't think so. So *you can't be unhappy about something that you don't **believe** you have to be unhappy about.*

4. Now in the case of Mrs. Thistlewood's pet worm, you know you don't want to lose any sleep over that, certainly not give up any joy or happiness you might be feeling. But, I can hear you saying, there is a whole range of other things that you will definitely get bent out of shape about. You just know that right? That is where belief comes in, because what you value or give meaning to is coded in your beliefs. And your beliefs are experienced by you as emotions in your body. Emotions are the experience of believing; they are beliefs in action and operation. So in the case of the deceased Freddy the worm, there is nothing that you believe such that you would feel an emotion such as sadness or grief. Obviously Mrs. Thistlewood includes Freddy as part of something she values and gives meaning to, so that is why she is so upset when she meets you in the street to tell you about it.

How does it happen that we come to value and give meaning to some things and not to others? Well, you know how. Your upbringing; the values your parents, teachers, friends and associates share. That's how you acquire the values and meanings that are packaged in your beliefs and felt as emotions. So while you wouldn't be upset over Freddy, you might well be over your favorite pet dog or cat, not to mention someone in your family or among your friends. They have meaning for you.

This response seems automatic doesn't it? That's why, when I laid out those ABC's in section 3, you probably had a hard time with "C." To feel bad when something you give value or meaning to is damaged, hurt or destroyed sure does seem natural.

While there are some common categories of beliefs that people tend to get upset about, (loss of people who have meaning, loss of things and social positions that have meaning and so on) the actual people and things do vary. Remember you couldn't get too upset about Freddy. Forget Freddy (sorry Mrs. Thistlewood), how about all the events in the newspaper or on television? Those thousand people or so who are always dying in some far away place don't have any specific meaning for you, they don't have names and faces that bring up values. So you usually don't get much beyond kind of mild sense of "gee, isn't that too bad," and wait for the sports and weather so you can get to bed. Now contrast that with how upset you may have become in the face of the 9/11 attack. Much closer to home, much more of a sense of being touched personally. But let's continue our focus for a moment longer on things that you don't feel connected with, at least anymore.

What about when your Aunt Rose   visits and begins to tell tales about you when you were a kid? You may find this especially embarrassing if *your* kids are around to listen to it. It seems remote and silly now to hear how you were absolutely in love with the boy next door to the point of tears and dramatics of great intensity when he did not return your interest. The guy turned out to be a real nerd that you wouldn't now give a second look to. Isn't that true? Or, what about the time you wanted to stay out late and finish that terrific game of stickball, but you had to come home. God, were you pissed!

You know the truth is that as you hear Aunt Rose tell these stories, you can scarcely remember any intensity at all. It means nothing. Zero. Zilch. What happened to all the emotional fireworks of days gone by? They are gone, that's what. Why? Because you have *changed your mind* along the way about what you value and give meaning to. Might there be some events that you still find evoke a strong emotional charge? Yes, and they are possible subjects for exploration with the Method, but in the vast majority of cases, what we have said here holds true.

This is a good place to begin with what I call "Exper/cises," short for experiential exercise. First I will usually give a few questions to answer, followed by one or more "exper/cises" for you to do. This is the beginning of your Joywork, so let's go. First I will give two questions which in this instance happen to be two of the three basic questions of the Option Method. They aim at identifying and refining your understanding of why you are unhappy about something in your life.

EXPER/CISE

Here, we will be dealing with things that you no longer have any emotional attachment to. In the spirit of Aunt Rose's stories of your childhood, consider some incidents from your past, about which you *have no present emotional connection*, but which you recall caused at least minor emotional firestorms when you were a kid. Use a photo album if you have it. I will be making this suggestion for other exper/cises later on as well.

As you review some typical instances of what I have asked for, use these two questions to identify and refine your understanding of what was going on for you at the time. One: ***What am I unhappy about?*** (In this case, "what was I") Make it as specific as you know how. Yes, yes, I know many years may have passed, but do the best you can. Don't worry. You can't fail at this Joywork. Once you have identified that, then ask yourself the second question: ***Why am I [was I] unhappy about that*** or alternatively, ***What about that (the thing I say I am unhappy about) "makes" me unhappy?***

Okay do this with as many instances as you can bring to mind. Write them out here so as to give them life and reality. This is a Workbook after all, so don't be afraid to mark it up. Use an accompanying note book as well. Contrary to what Sister Mary Diptheria may have told you in the first grade, (or old Mrs. Schnitzelbeak if you were not in parochial school the way I was) books are meant to be written in. Your thoughts are as important as the thoughts of the person you are reading, at least to you. So let her rip!

Okay, so you have done that. Great. What was the point? Simple. To show you that you *do* change your mind about what you believe and that when you do, your emotions follow like little goslings after the mother goose. Was it natural for you to be upset in the ways you were upset at age six or ten or fifteen? Well it was "natural" only in the sense that given what you believed, it made sense that you would respond in the ways you did. Now, once you no longer believe that, there is no emotional response to be found. Conclusion: ***what you believe is what you feel. Period!*** Outside of beliefs, there are no emotions to be found. Now of course there is a human "startle reflex" and other neurological responses that we will discuss a bit more later, so obviously, you do have "feelings" of a physiological nature when the boundaries of your body are crossed either by actually being touched or by triggering one of the body's early warning systems. That is not what we are talking about here, okay. I am speaking only of emotions which are rooted in your perceptions and then through the process of giving value and meaning, they are deposited in a pattern of beliefs.

5. So we have established that beliefs are experienced in the body as emotions; that we can change our beliefs and that when we do our emotions will absolutely correspond to that change. So far so good. But you may be asking: "okay, but what about the speed at which I seem to respond to things? There hardly seems time to alter my responses when everything just seems to tumble out of me. Somebody scratches my brand new car and I get pissed. I learn my dear Aunt Sally has cancer, I cry." Yes, yes I know that. What we are aiming for here is to help you, first, to decide whether you want your joy and happiness more fully in your life and, second, to demonstrate to you that it is possible to have them if you want them.

Now as to the speed of responses, not to worry. It has to be that way because otherwise we would never get anything done. So in each and every moment of our lives we are responding to what is happening with our own thoughts and with the actions and events of the people and things in the world. Despite the speed of our responses, we ourselves were the ones who put together the meanings and values that created the belief, then the emotion. This doesn't mean that we don't control our beliefs so as have that particular response. It is a matter of using the Option questions to identify what we believe and thereby putting ourselves in the position to change or alter that belief if we so choose.

Now the really interesting thing is that so often we actually do not choose to change or alter a belief that produces unhappy feelings. Ah, now that is more what is at the heart of things than anything else. I can hear you saying to me: "Hey, you mean I shouldn't get pissed when someone scratches my new car? How is anyone to know I don't like that if I don't vent my feelings about it? Answer me that, smart guy! Feeling joy now would be stupid because it would sap me of my resolve to get the jerk who did this and make him responsible." Or: "Hey you mean I shouldn't cry when my Aunt Sally gets cancer? What kind of an unfeeling slob do you think I am? Maybe you have been watching too much *Startrek* and have a "Mr. Spock complex" or something. When someone I care about is hurt or in pain, I am damn sure going to show that I care. Joy has no place at this time. It would show a disgraceful lack of empathy and sincerity to feel good when someone you love feels bad. God, Frank, that's just so elemental. Get with the program, pahleeezze!"

The point is that joy is not joy to you and happiness is not happiness to you if you take it to mean that you have to go against your values and what you hold dear to experience it. Of course. Actually this is a great place to introduce the last of the three Option questions to complete the core of the Method you can use to let go of as much unhappiness as you find reasonable to let go of. It echoes the apparent dilemma that we have just experienced: ***What are you afraid would happen (or would it mean*** *anything about you) if you were not unhappy about that (that is whatever it is you have identified as being what you are unhappy about)?*

Do you see? What you are dealing with many times is the fear that, if you are not unhappy at appropriate times and circumstances, it will indeed mean something negative about you. Well, what can we do about it? First, let's start by making a distinction that can be critical for you in letting go of unhappiness. That is that *I am not asking you to be happy about the things that occur that you have no affection for in life*, such as scratches on your new car or the illness of those you love, or loss of job, or problems with your children or spouse, or any of the endless events and experiences that you do not want to happen to you or others. No, of course not. What I am saying is that *you can find it possible to be happy even though there are things going on that you don't like!* The key here is understanding that your happiness and joy do not represent a betrayal of your caring, loving concern for anyone else. Nor are we in any way talking about a surrender of your capacity to pursue remuneration from, or punishment of those who may be responsible for having done harm to you, or those you love. You recall that you did not find it necessary to be miserable or pained to any considerable degree over the news events of misfortunes in places far away. Of course as I mentioned earlier, you will reply that in such a case those events did not have a personal face on them; that is, you did not give them any meaning or value such that you would require unhappiness of yourself about them. But what is clear is that the mere knowledge of misfortune is not enough, normally speaking, to draw forth a response of unhappiness from you, is it? Not for most of you I don't think (we will talk more to this point later on). Let's review what we have learned to this point:

REVIEW: Sections One through Five

1. You do want your happiness but

2. You don't believe it is possible *not* to be unhappy

3. The ABC's tell us that   A/There is just you and the world
B/You don't control the world
C/ You do control the attitude you construct toward whatever the world presents to you at any given moment.

4. While "C" is yet to be proven to you, you understand that *you can't be unhappy about something you don't believe you have to be unhappy about.* Further you know from Aunt Rose's childhood tales that you change your mind about what you value and believe and that, when you do, your feelings about those things change. So *what you believe is what you feel.*

5. You are not being asked to be happy about things you do not want to be happy about, but it is being suggested that you can be happy even though there are things you do not like going on at any time.

Additionally, you have been given the Option Questions:

What am I unhappy about?

Why am I unhappy, i.e., what about the thing I say I am unhappy about "makes" me unhappy?

What am I afraid would happen (or would it mean anything about me) if I were not unhappy about that?

CHAPTER TWO

THE QUESTIONS

6. THE OPTION QUESTIONS.

Let's take a closer look at the Option Questions. Remember, you can find whole dialogue examples of their use in both *Joywords,* in other materials I may have published, but let me illustrate their usage for you here once more to intensify your orientation and the likelihood you will use them.

QUESTION ONE:

WHAT AM I UNHAPPY ABOUT?

Specify, make it concrete: I am unhappy about my job, about my wife, about my husband, about not having the money or position I want, about being ill. Be aware of the way in which merely asking the question sets the course for a journey out of pain and distress. Write down your responses to this question for your personal journal. Again, the more specific and contextually relevant you make those questions, the more they will begin to come alive in the unfolding of the Option Method. It is always okay to ask a clarifying question such as "What do I mean?" if you are puzzled by what you come up with as something you say you are unhappy about. Actually, the second Option Method question will help greatly in this regard.

QUESTION TWO:

WHY AM I UNHAPPY ABOUT THAT? OR WHAT ABOUT THAT (THE THING I SAY I AM UNHAPPY ABOUT) "MAKES" ME UNHAPPY?

Yes, you may suspect even now that nothing "makes" you unhappy, but when you are experiencing unhappiness, that is the discomforting emotions that come as a result of your beliefs, it does feel as if it were the truth; that is, it feels as if you were the object of something or someone that created unhappiness in you. How could it be otherwise? You have to feel what you believe according to your values, or you wouldn't feel anything at all. Remember what we learned earlier *that what you believe is what you feel.* Feelings, in the sense we have spoken of as experiences arising from our perceptions and then judgments as to what those perceptions mean to us, can come from no other source! No one feels unhappy unless they are congruent with the belief that there is something to feel unhappy about. You will notice as well that this will set off a sequence of "things" that "make" you unhappy as you follow your belief trail. As this trail unfolds, you may be able to extinguish the belief right at this point merely by exposing the belief pattern underlying the unhappiness you begin with.

From your answers to question #1, write down your answers (beliefs) to question #2. Examples: The lack of money makes me unhappy; the lack of attention from my spouse makes me unhappy; the lack of recognition from my boss makes me unhappy; the lack of good health makes me unhappy etc., etc. Take plenty of time: it's all for you! Now when you have done that, **DO IT AGAIN!** That's right, keep asking yourself the second question. You know why? Because what you say makes you unhappy is not actually what makes you unhappy. There almost always is yet another  layer of people, things, occasions that lie behind what you originally begin with as having identified as the person place or thing that makes you unhappy. Let me give you an "Aunt Rose" example:

Q: Why does Aunt Rose make me unhappy?

A: Because when I was a kid she made me eat lasagna, crusty bread and olives.

Q: What about that makes you unhappy?

A: 'Cause now I actually like lasagna, crusty bread and olives.

Q: And what about that makes you unhappy?

A: 'Cause I went from being a skinny kid that weighed 70 pounds to a real heavyweight that tips the scales at 260 pounds.

Q: And what about that makes you unhappy?

A: 'Cause poor old Aunt Rose just died?

Q: And what about that makes you unhappy?

A: 'Cause she forgot to give me the recipe for her lasagna before she died.

Well, okay, you begin to get the idea. Just like Aunt Rose's lasagna, there are any number of layers to your beliefs about your unhappiness. There are any number of clarifying questions that you can ask to help keep you on track with what you believe makes you unhappy. For example, in addition to the question cited above in the First Option Question "What do I mean ?" you can ask "Why do I believe that?" i.e., "Why do I believe I have to be unhappy about losing my job?" Additionally you could ask "What would be the worst thing about losing my job," or "What would I be most frightened about in losing my job etc.?" You will find yourself pulling up more material that way and penetrating more deeply into the heart of your unhappy beliefs.

QUESTION THREE:

WHAT AM I AFRAID WOULD HAPPEN (OR WOULD IT MEAN ANYTHING ABOUT ME) IF I WERE NOT UNHAPPY ABOUT THAT (WHATEVER I HAVE IDENTIFIED AS BEING WHAT I AM UNHAPPY ABOUT)?

Here is the question that comes when you run out of "reasons" to be unhappy and confess that you don't know why. Even Aunt Rose's lasagna has a limited number of layers after all. This question usually is asked at the end of a trail of "what about that" questions when you reach a dead end in the belief path. There then can be a ripeness for this question (just like a summer tomato begging for some olive oil and basil) in the sense that you may be open to seeing how it isn't any "thing" that is making you unhappy. The feeling comes from your belief that you must be unhappy about a particular issue because that is a way to avoid the judgments of others and of yourself about you. Did you get that? *Avoid the judgments of others.* Just take a minute to take that in. You don't want to be seen as a schmuck for being a way others might not approve of. Unhappiness is also a way of attempting to make sure that you do or do not do something. It is an internal "twisting of your arm" to act as a reminder or a constraint.

Remember when you were a kid, or at least I remember that we would joke around by twisting our own arms behind our backs as if we were being made to do something we really did want to do (like chow down on a massive plate of Aunt Rose's lasagna. And, eat your heart out, cause I actually do have the recipe under lock and key).

Well, while that was how we fooled around as kids, in truth, we actually do as I just described. We "internally" twist our arms to be the way we think (and we think others think) we are supposed to be.

But, let's look more closely to see how we might arrive at that understanding. Now asking this third question is difficult for people starting out with the Option Method because the knee jerk response is so often, "Well, gee if I wasn't unhappy about [losing my job, having bad health, not having my wife's love etc] then I would be happy of course." So initially it may seem to make no sense at all, or be totally counter intuitive to what it seems you are trying to accomplish, which is to get rid of your unhappiness. In other words, the question may seem to be asking "Why not just be happy!" Most people will shrug their shoulders and say, hey, that's why I'm here because I can't seem to be happy and there is some reason that keeps me from being happy." Ah ha! Precisely! What you will come to know, and know somehow already without articulating it, is that your unhappiness is not somehow supernaturally or neurophysiologically imposed upon you. You have your reasons. The first two questions have delved into and elaborated in perhaps great detail what they are. Now you basically have run out of reasons that you can find and up pops this third question. The question assumes that there are reasons and is not just a way of simply urging you to be happy without resolving those reasons. So, give yourself here the gift of patience. Take a deep breath, and as best you can open yourself up to the true nature of what is being asked. When you do then you may begin to find responses that are more in the range of "It would mean that I don't care about myself," or "It would prove that I am really just bad for myself," or "It would mean that I really don't want what I keep protesting to you and myself that I want," or "I'd be plain crazy if I were not to be unhappy about that," or "What a cold uncaring character I would be not to be unhappy about that, this would only prove what I fear and others have said that I am essentially toxic and bad for myself," etc..

Okay, now we are getting somewhere. Once your responses are genuinely, and in a heartfelt manner emerging with that kind of response pattern, you are just kissing the goal of unlocking the door to the dungeon of your beliefs in unhappiness. Additionally, you may find yourself answering: "Well, if I weren't unhappy about not losing my job, then I would have no motivation to be diligent in trying to find new employment," or "If I were not unhappy about not having my wife's love, then it would mean that I really did not love her," or "If I were not unhappy about my ill health then I would not be moved to do something about it." Okay, another crucial layer of the purpose of unhappiness is exposed. Unhappiness is seen as necessary to motivate us to avoid even greater unhappiness. The question we can ask ourselves is something like: "Am I saying that my way of making sure that I know that I do want to do something about [unemployment, sickness, wife's love, etc.] is to make myself unhappy so that I will be sure to be motivated to take care of myself?" Alright, so that reveals several uses of unhappiness: first, again, as a motivator to get us to do what we say we want to do but don't trust we can do without unhappiness as a spur to get us to do it; second, thereby we avoid the greater unhappiness of confirming that we are really bad for ourselves if we don't act to do something about our problems. Bingo! If you arrive here through a genuine, experientially congruent feeling path as you ask those questions, you will now be feeling a readiness for the exhilaration of having your happiness in this moment. Use these questions for a knock-out punch: "Why would it mean I would be crazy?" or "Why would it mean I would be bad for myself or my happiness if I were not unhappy about that?" or "Since I know that the unhappiness I'm focusing on now has not served me well, and only actually brought more unhappiness, and, since I know I really want my happiness, then how would embracing and allowing myself to experience happiness now be in any way a betrayal of anything I cherish and hold dear?" Step out of the darkness of your assumptions and suspicions about yourself and embrace the light of the truth of your happiness and you are home! How does it feel? If you still are struggling, that's fine, just keep an open mind, treat yourself with compassion, give yourself the gift of hope and focus back on the questions. A great treasure awaits you for your labors.

Let's do an "exper/cise" that may help bring this concept to life:

EXPER/CISE:

With the help of *Joywords*, [and in particular the dialogues which give good examples of how to employ these questions] along with any of my other published material, begin to trace out some of the patterns of your beliefs. Start with simple things for this exper/cise, because we will be delving into a whole host of themes in the sections on unhappiness and happiness. For example, you got angry because your two year old dropped her Popsicle in the supermarket. Now you can get in touch with how you might be afraid that others would judge you because in their opinion you couldn't control your child and you made a mess. So being angry? Can you begin to see how that anger serves the purpose of showing you mean business, that you don't like the situation you are in, that by golly you are going to show your kid (and the folks watching) who's in charge, etc?

Or when the new guy screwed up at work and you joined with some of the "old timers" in judging the guy as a jerk. Isn't it true that you were "following the crowd" in that instance and were afraid that not judging the new guy, not joining in the chorus of criticism might have left you open to being criticized yourself? Hmmmm?

Or you get on the scale and Oh my God, too much of Aunt Rose's lasagna! You are upset, a bit depressed, pissed at yourself. You can't trust yourself around food. Wow. Now can you get in touch with how not being unhappy in that way might be perceived by you, yes you, as opening yourself to becoming even more uncontrolled in your eating habits? So the misery seems important to have. Well, that's how it seems. Then pick some instances of the type I have just described and apply the third question. See how many times you can arrive at a clear understanding of you using your unhappiness to keep yourself in line or in conformity with what others expect of you and what you may expect of yourself. Give it a try.

Let yourself gradually open up to the potentially awesome liberation that is resident in this question. As you develop greater fluency in questioning yourself, you are going to be making more and more breakthroughs to the truth about unhappiness: that it is a made up constraint put in place ostensibly to avoid even greater unhappiness.

CHAPTER THREE

KEY CONCEPTS

7. SOME KEY CONCEPTS

Now that you have used the Option Questions a bit and perhaps gone through some of the other material that may be available as noted in the introduction to become comfortable with how the Method works, please consider the following informational sections that will aid you in deepening your confidence that you can have your joy NOW. Read carefully, answer the questions and do the experiential exercises. Please refer back to earlier explanations whenever something is not clear. This is the advantage of the **Joybuilding System:** it gives you different modalities to help deepen your understanding and readiness to embrace your joy. Take all the time you want to write down and savor your responses. Use the Option Method to demythologize any beliefs that may be exposed as you ponder those responses. Write each response down with as much exactitude as you feel is warranted until you are satisfied and ready to move on to the next one. Remember. This is for you alone, to be shared with you alone (though you may work in a group should that suit you, as well). Thus the generosity of your openness and truthfulness can be as unlimited as you feel comfortable allowing it to be. I invite you to the freedom of utter truthfulness in complete support of yourself.

BELIEF

We have already underlined the key role of belief in Sections 3, 4, and 5, but because it is so central we really can't overdo our emphasis on it. Belief is important to understand in order to see how unhappiness arises. A belief is what a person assumes or holds to be true. It is a matter of opinion, the opinion of that person about that particular matter. Emotions follow from our beliefs; they are the experience of believing; they are beliefs in action and operation. We have seen how Mrs. Thistlewood reacted to the demise of Freddy the Worm; we have done exper/cises that demonstrated how we reacted to things in the past, but have lost that emotional connection because we have changed our minds about those incidents over time.

Essentially, then, our emotions are the expression of our beliefs about the causes of happiness and unhappiness. Right? Our car gets scratched, we get pissed. We are experiencing the result of our decision that our car getting scratched is a reason to be distressed. The speed at which it takes place blurs the intricacy of the whole process, but it does not change the fact that what we believe (for example, a scratched new car is the occasion to be pissed, i.e., unhappy) is what we feel! It does not matter whether you are talking about moods or attitudes or moral judgments. They all are the same thing. The central understanding is that we choose our emotions by believing what we believe and so we feel happy or unhappy according to what we believe. Nothing "causes" unhappiness: no person, event, thing, no misfired neuron, genetic inclination, developmental experience or lack of same. It isn't Freddy the Worm's death, or the scratched car, or Aunt Sally's cancer (and certainly not Aunt Rose's lasagna, though a bit of gastric agita might occur at times) that creates unhappiness in you. It is your belief that these events have to be the occasion for unhappiness that creates the unhappiness in the form of whatever feeling follows from that interpretation: anger, sadness, frustration, etc. Unhappiness is the belief in unhappiness experienced and operating as the feeling.

Now, on the other hand we already know that there is no way that we can become unhappy about something we do not believe we have to be unhappy about. How many of you are unhappy about vanilla ice cream? (Now, pistachio, that's another story!) Absurd for most of you I am sure, but you get the point here. There are things in our experience about which unhappiness is simply not relevant. Conversely, you are unhappy only when you believe there **is** something to be unhappy about. Therefore, our emotions are judgments, that is interpretations, about whether something is going to be "good" or "bad" for our own personal happiness. Thus when we judge something to be good, we are happy immediately at that prospect. When we judge something to be bad, we are immediately unhappy at that prospect. If you have the winning lotto ticket, you don't wait until you get the check before you are rejoicing about it, right? Conversely, if you get what you consider bad news, Aunt Sally's cancer, or a pink slip on your job, you are immediately unhappy. Our emotions are evaluations expressing our beliefs. Hopefully this is crystal clear for you at this point. If not, review the material. Always a good thing to do. After all, coming to understand this is for you, for your greater joy, so be generous to yourself. This is an admonition I will repeat.

FEAR

Fear is central to the understanding of how unhappiness arises. Yes, yes, it is *belief* that is the unhappiness alive in our bodies as the emotion we are feeling, sadness, anger, frustration, hatred etc. But we can manifest believing in two ways.

1. We can actually experience something that we instantly interpret, according to our beliefs, as something to be unhappy about. When Mrs. Thistlewood came upon the fearsome sparrow (a serial worm slayer no doubt sufficient to put Dr. Hannibal Lecter to shame) savaging Freddy, she was instantly unhappy according to her beliefs right in that moment, on the spot. That's the first situation in which unhappiness arises, and it is true that fear in some form is never absent from unhappiness.

2. But by far the more pervasive, chronic sense of unhappiness in all its forms is probably this second type which comes under the heading of *Anticipating Unhappiness!*

Fear enters in here in a primary way because it is at this point we believe that something *will* make us unhappy. Got that? That is precisely what fear is, the belief that we are helpless before some assumed event that has the power to make us unhappy. For example, my living in dread that Aunt Rose will die and not leave me a detailed recipe on how to make her lasagna! Now that is dread! **Note**: the thing feared *has not yet happened! Fear is the feeling state that corresponds to the belief that we will have to be unhappy about some person place or thing in our future.* Note the sequence: you are feeling discomforting/unhappy feelings in your body **now**, in anticipation that you **will** have to (or might have to) feel discomforting/unhappy feelings in your body at some time in the **future!** You feel the feeling now (just like the lotto ticket or Aunt Sally's cancer examples) because the unhappiness is the feeling/belief of anticipated distress which becomes our unhappiness now. Now is the only time we can feel anything at all. We will be looking at categories of unhappiness and see how fear plays the major role in unhappiness.

EXPER/CISE

If this section is not obvious to you then try this simple test. Imagine that you just were informed by a reliable source that you won ten million dollars. Would you wait until you had the check in your hand or would you feel immediately elated?

Again, imagine you have been informed by a reliable source that you have a fatal disease and little time to live. Would you wait for the signs and symptoms of the disease to manifest strongly before you reacted or would you immediately have a strong response?

So your responses are based on decisions made in this instant and derive directly from beliefs about how these events will affect you in the future. If you believe that they are things to be happy or unhappy about, that is how you will feel *now.* In the unhappy scenario, you don't see any way to experience the event otherwise. It just seems to require or create the unhappy feelings and additionally you feel the dread of even greater unhappiness in the future. In the happy scenario, most people are convinced by the information of having won the money that they have permission to feel happy now in anticipation of even greater happiness in the future. Of course I hope that as you do your Joywork, you will come to appreciate that your happiness is not dependant upon the gains and losses of your existence. But let's travel further and open up more understanding to get you to that point.

FEAR /DREAD OF LOSS OF FREEDOM: THAT IS HELPLESSNESS

Now, one of the direct outcomes of instantly feeling the emotions of unhappiness, both as a direct response to some event, or in anticipation of being faced with responding to some person place or thing in the hypothetical realm called the future, is that we can easily come to believe that we don't control how we feel. The degree to which we actually feel our emotions to be out of control in various circumstances is the degree to which our fear turns into the more intense form of fear called dread. Now, remember the ABC's of happiness and unhappiness.

A/ there is just you and the world;

B/ you don't control the world;

C/ you do control the attitude you take toward what the world presents to you in any given moment.

Remember I told you that since you probably didn't fully believe in "C" that then the area of most difficulty would revolve around "B" right? Well, here we are guys, smack in the middle of "B" country, the world that we don't control. Now, if we believe that the best we can do is passively observe how the world presents us with "horrific" situations to which we have no choice but to respond with painful feelings, then this will be the main arena of our fear and dread, right? Even if we have some modified, moderate control, there still remain whole areas where we will be helpless before the events the world *may* present to us. Ah, you see… much is in that word "may." A whole bunch of anticipatory fear or anxiety can be constructed from potential scenarios we derive from the tales of our parents (i.e., the context of our upbringing), the books we read, the media avalanche of near apocalyptically tinged information that swamps us each and every day.

As you can imagine, the events of 9/11 and the psychology that has followed those events have added a substantial load to the general anticipatory dread in our world. The sense for Americans that we controlled at least our corner of the globe and were somehow immune to the destructive potentials of those unhappy people who follow some fanatical, fundamentalist vision of life, was shattered. Indeed we do not control the world. And those who would drive a deep wedge into our everyday equanimity know well that nothing is more corrosive, divisive and destructive of the social fabric of a nation than dread. To freeze the minds and spirits of a people is to either to break their spirit or to create a counter reaction of rage and punishing responses that will eventually return as guilt and regret for many. So, all of these circumstances become part of how the emerging human being forms a perspective of their world.

How this information is given value and weight in our families as we grow up tends to be incorporated by us into an interpretive framework or prism for viewing the world. So, we arrive at a central concept that itself derives from the belief called fear, which in turn is a derivative of the basic belief in unhappiness. Fear causes us to believe that ***that we can be made unhappy against our will***. Now you know what that feels like. You think about getting some fatal disease and you just know, given what you believe, that you will be terrified. You think about being laid off and you again anticipate how terrible that is going to feel. You think about your spouse leaving you or having an affair and you immediately taste some of the misery that you anticipate feeling should that happen. If I were to ask you whether you wanted to feel unhappy about any or all of those things, many of you would feel mystified by the question. No, you might say, but what choice would you have, you might reply. The unhappiness just seems to be there, waiting for the event to unfold to seize your senses with the painful emotions.

Well, you can see how this would scare the "bedoodles" out of you, right?

First, of course, if we accept this idea, it would make our choosing irrelevant! Decisions about being happy or unhappy would, in a great number of important instances (which will vary with each and every one of you) simply not belong to you. So, no matter what we believed otherwise, if we believe that there are powers or agencies within[*] or outside ourselves that have the capability to overrule our own desires to be happy for ourselves, then that is ultimately dread and unhappiness. In such a scenario we would be but pawns and victims of these mysterious agencies and could only wait in trembling anxiety for an eruption of misery as a result of these forces we do not control. What we have done in this scenario is to take the "B" of the ABC's ("You don't control the world") and ***include all of "you"***

---

[*] As we will see a bit later, this is a belief in unconscious forces, urges, needs, that force us to act against our values, against our will, to be ways we do not want to be or ways we fear to be.

in the world, not just your physiology, but the very essence of who you are. So in truth, "**You**" disappear and become just a mere object in the world to be acted upon and moved around, not just as it pertains to your physical body (which is certainly a part of the world) but as it pertains to you, the very *"what it feels like to be you experience" that is the core of who you are.* This is the real origin of our concept of evil and dread of being evil which I talk about at length in *The Unbearable Wrongness of Being*, as well as other places. So, scratch the car, I am unhappy. Aunt Sally's cancer, I am unhappy. (Yes, yes, I know, there are some "unhappinesses" that seem so appropriate and compassionate. We will deal with that just ahead.) Lose a job, I am unhappy. Now **remember please**, we are not asking you to be happy about those things, but following the distinction we made earlier in Section 5, only that you consider whether these situations **require** your unhappiness. In the scenario we are now reviewing, there are a bunch of instances where you may believe that you have no choice.

REVIEW: To repeat, our attitudes are forged out of beliefs that we assume and affirm over a period of time about happiness and unhappiness. Once affirmed they come into play instantly according to our understanding of them as relevant to a particular occasion. However, because of the speed of the application of the attitudinal response, it *seems* as if they have a life of their own and, again, that we are victims of interior unconscious forces responding automatically to exterior cues. This way of believing puts you squarely in "B" country of the ABC's. Here you are at the mercy of forces in the world over which you have no control. Here, the "world" also includes a big chunk of you, your physiology, your interior life, the very core of who your are, because unhappiness erupts out of yourself **it would seem** in non-volitional response to what the world presents to you.

Solution: in this scenario, following the logic of "B" alone there is no solution. You have literally lost yourself and are adrift in a sea of material causality and cryptic forces you do not control. You either find a way to control the world (drugs that regulate your brain physiology, therapeutic exorcisms that get the "devil" of unhappiness out of you, technological wonders that tame the world and bend it to your will, or just plain miracles that come magically from powers outside yourself) or you are in deep existential doo doo. Even Aunt Rose's sausage with brocolli rabe won't help you. Only by coming to understand you and the world through the vision of the "C" scenario, the one presented in this book, could you come to know that what you say you are unhappy about does not make you unhappy. What you fear has the power to make you unhappy does not make you unhappy. Rather the belief that it can make you unhappy is what makes you unhappy and *that alone*.

8. THE "HAPPINESS" THAT IS NOT HAPPINESS: HAPPINESS AS SOMETHING WRONG FOR YOU

Okay, now let us take on another notion that can cause confusion. Recall a few sentences ago at the end of Section 7 I noted that some forms of unhappiness seemed very natural and even desirable. Also in Section 5, after you "blasted" me for suggesting that you might not have to be unhappy about particular situations, remember I said that "happiness is not happiness if you take it to mean that you have to go against your values and what you hold dear to experience it." So now you know the meaning of this section heading. The concept of happiness is often confused with unhappiness in the sense that we believe that to be happy in certain ways and under certain conditions would actually bring us unhappiness. Again, why? Because it would go against our values. Thus we fear what we mistakenly call happiness.

Should we experience this "happiness" we may believe that we will lose our moral bearings and become bad people. Culture demands our allegiance to certain experiences of unhappiness as pledges of our loyalty to the values represented by being unhappy in certain situations. Not to be unhappy would be seen as a violation of that loyalty and hence a threat to the sense of community and socialization that is so important to identify individuals as "good" citizens or persons. We see this in the ethnic and religious strife that is so pervasive at this time, where former neighbors in Yugoslavia who lived together for years in peace despite their ethnic/religious differences, suddenly became mortal enemies when their values became closely identified with their own ethnic or religious backgrounds. Outrage and hatreds are expected as we saw in the phenomenon of the Taliban in Afghanistan and anyone who would counsel otherwise is seen as a traitor to their group.

What we so often believe is that if we are happy we will abandon all our commitments to people, that we will not care for ourselves, that we will therefore be out of our minds and worse still "evil" not to be unhappy about certain situations (what are described as tragedies, losses, affronts to moral customs or cultural norms etc.). Now, what fits the model of things to be appropriately unhappy about does vary from culture to culture and indeed from individual to individual depending upon what was most highly valued in our family surroundings and subsequently what we made our own value system.

For example, while I might get away with saying that being angry about scratching your car is a matter of choice, I will get blasted when I speak about matters closer to the core of what we treasure: our parents, children, our jobs, our physical health, the well being of our society, violations of our laws, especially when a situation ends up causing physical injury or death, and most central, although not always acknowledged as such, harm or mortal injury to ourselves. Indeed, not to get unhappy is described often in pathological terms as "denial" or as a moral or even genetic defect of some sort. In any case such a withholding of the prescribed experience will, it is asserted from this perspective, lead to unhappiness of some kind at a later date. In other words, **you will pay for not being unhappy**. It will be either a physical ailment, or psychological deficit, or if all other things fail, then God will punish you for not being the way you were supposed to be at the time you were supposed to be that way! (And if God doesn't get you, Mrs. Thistlewood will for even suggesting that she has a choice about grieving over Freddy the Worm.) Here the specter noted in my book the *Unbearable Wrongness of Being* is raised, the specter of being "bad for yourself," or against some hypothesized "authentic" or true self.

But the "running amok" "craziness" often associated with lack of unhappiness is merely a straw man, that is it is just a "scare" tactic to keep us and all others in line. As described by those who purvey this notion, i.e., moralists, psychologists or other cultural gatekeepers, such states are not happiness at all, but caricatures of states of happiness that have been distorted to present an unappetizing perspective and to ward off those who would stray from the conventions of the community about how we are to feel. I am going to give some more detailed examples ahead in the Section of *Fear of Being Bad For Ourselves*, but here is an example that seems somewhat amusing to me now from my own past.

I remember being an "altar boy" in a Catholic school, where I was to serve along with many of my fellows at the midnight mass of Christmas. Excited by the arrival of Christmas, my friend and I were kidding around in the sacristy shortly before the ceremony was to begin and we were roundly yelled at by a combination of Fr. McBother and Sister Mary Diptheria for demonstrating a shameful lack of proper seriousness at this solemn time. Whereupon we were both dispatched from the service and deprived of our "altar boy" status. Our joy and excitement at Christmas time was "inappropriately" manifested in this context. Yes, yes, I understand that according to their lights the adults acted as expected. The point here is that an attempt was made to make us feel shamed by the expression of our joy, an attempt which, I am happy to report, was largely unsuccessful. The good order of society and the practical procedures required to carry out the way our world runs do require our attention, particularly if we might endanger ourselves with a lack of attention (no fooling around when your physical well being is at stake, such as on a high ladder, or piloting an airplane etc.). But we can be joyfully attentive and focused on the practical issues of our existence; we don't have to surrender our joy to someone else's version of the solemnity of the moment.

EXPER/CISE

- Recall instances of where you were reprimanded for being "inappropriately" happy in your life. Think about your present experiences. Do you feel any constraints on being happy or do you feel uncomfortable with the happiness you may be allowing yourself to have? Do you begrudge happiness to others (the neighbor that you don't like is having a good time at his barbecue; a politician that you can't stand is on TV being shown on vacation with a smiling face etc.)? See the degree to which you can allow your own and others good feelings. Use the Method and record your success.

EMBRACING MISERY

It happens the other way as well. We are told that being unhappy is actually good for us. "No pain, no gain" is a contemporary slogan. Our unhappiness, our show of painful emotions, our demonstrations of appropriate anger and righteousness at those who violate our covenants (including ourselves) become the public demonstration and the private evidence to ourselves, that we are actually for what we are for (that is, what is "good") and against what we are against (that is, what is "bad"). Without these personal emotional discomfitures, we have come to believe, we have no point of reference. In other words, if we don't kick ourselves in the butt or have others kick us in the butt, we won't know enough to go after what we want or avoid what we don't want. We have all seen sports figures get angry at themselves when they miss a shot, Tiger Woods, Michael Jordan etc. We just have to go to the local little league to see how the kids imitate the same unhappiness when they fail to perform up to their own and oth ers' expectations. We can perhaps remember- I know I do- being urged to be ashamed of our behaviors, to feel bad about ourselves as a way of molding our behavior and avoiding even greater infractions. Thus were we encouraged to embrace pain and unhappiness as a good thing to remind us of our need to follow the rules and constraints of family and society.

In this way unhappiness is raised to the level of a communal sacrament that all must partake of in order to prove they are worthy, caring, loving, sane, compassionate and moral people. Those who do not drink from the chalice of sorrows are suspect at a minimum as eccentric, or feared at worst as somehow potential sociopaths.

But we could know what we value without sorrow as a guide. When we first behold our children born, we know we love them not out of sorrow or pain, but out of the irrepressible joy of the awesomeness of life appearing so intimately in our midst. Listening to great music, hugging your spouse, taking in the beauty of a breathtaking landscape, doing that extra special thing that you know will please someone you love: do these require our pain to know we want to do them? When we lose someone to death, we have not lost that value of them or the knowledge of our love for them. Grief or sorrow adds nothing to that value or knowledge. While we attend to the duties of expressing our pain at their no longer being with us, it keeps us from the joy of remembrance.

But what has happened is a variant of not getting what you want and being unhappy about that, a fundamental problem with "B" of the ABC's, i.e.: **You don't control the world** (more on that just below). Why? Because the world does not always cooperate in responding to our attempts to get what we want. Hey, if you haven't noticed that by this point in your life, then even Aunt Rose's special Calimari with super hot pepper sauce won't revive you. What we value does not always happen for us; that includes the maintenance in life of those we love. When things do not conform to what we value, we are not against ourselves if we do not become upset. We are not schmucks or unfeeling clods. We could know in our hearts what we love and what we do not like without constantly reminding ourselves by sticking the "pins" of unhappiness in our butts. That is what your *Joywork* in this book is offering to teach you. Our happiness never has to be touched by our failure to successfully realize our values in the world by having things be the way we want them to be. So even if Aunt Sally has cancer, even if we don't get the promotion, even if our kids decide to be rock stars instead of doctors, even if we don't possess the good health we would want, we can still realize our joy on an ongoing basis. We will delve into all this in more depth as we go on, so stay with me.

THE DREAD OF NOT GETTING WHAT WE WANT

Okay, so I mentioned in the last section the problem in the realm of "B" with not getting what you want. Let's talk a bit about the confusion of wanting and needing. *Wanting* comes from freedom, the freedom to affirm what we like in the world, the freedom to pursue our preferences with zest and gusto. It represents the wonderful associative flow of our playing in the world. We can move easily and comfortably through a whole series of wants without experiencing any threat to our equanimity by their fulfillment or lack of fulfillment. Whoa, I can hear you saying. That is precisely **not** how I experience wanting. Well, right, since most of us have lost touch with that original sense of ease in our wanting, we now believe that there are ways of being that are necessary in order for us to be happy or avoid unhappiness. We describe these states as *"needs"*, meaning *that without which happiness is impossible or unhappiness is unavoidable.* So when we want something, that something is not required in order for us to be happy; but when we say we need something, then we have made having it a requirement in order for us to be happy.

Once we do that we have lost our freedom to want without dread. Wanting now becomes problematic and fraught with difficulties. First, we may not always get what we want and if we make the wanting a "need" either in the personal sense or in the sense that the community approves of, we are left helpless before the momentum of our beliefs which bring us unhappiness when we do not get what we want. Look, I may want a plate of Aunt Rose's lasagna (I can't think of a time when I don't), but if I say I need one (which my wife says I definitely do not) then I set myself up for unhappiness when I don't get it, right?

Second, we may want what we believe that we are not supposed to want and find ourselves "needing" things that are "bad" or "evil." Feelings of compulsion, obsessions or "urges" often describe this situation of personal, "unauthorized needs" as we will describe it in a Section ahead. Because of the way we put ourselves together out of the world of our families and society growing up, we may have allowed only some very constrained, narrow pathways for feeling good to squeeze some very diluted joy out of life. So, for example, we may use food as a pathway and find ourselves overstuffed and overweight like one of Aunt Rose's *panini* or super sandwiches; we feel we "need" the food for some moments of satisfaction, but we also fear this "need" because it brings with it unwanted consequences. Often we may seek out people and keep people in our lives who we feel we "need" rather than love. The consequences of such relationships may be negative or even physically dangerous. You begin to see the way we have constructed a "bind" for ourselves, right? We begin to fear ourselves as vehicles on a collision course with what we believed were our own values as well as the values of the culture. We may see ourselves as "evil," which is of course the *primal dread* I describe in the *Unbearable Wrongness of Being*. We may experience our freedom as a burden, because out of that dreaded freedom we choose to be against ourselves by somehow "choosing" or "needing" things that are not good for us. Better, as the Russian novelist and philosopher, Dostoevsky said in the words of his "Grand Inquisitor," to be without freedom, than to live free in dread of the possibility of becoming evil through the exercise of it.

This fear of ourselves and how our wants, now turned into needs, might be destructive to us has spawned elaborate answers in the history of human thought. In the East, whole cultures have created systems whereby the self and its desires have become the culprit in creating suffering. What has to be sacrificed is precisely human individuality to escape the apparent insoluble dilemma. What science and sociology has done is to try and demonstrate that we are not at all free, but just "meat machines," creatures of genetics, the software of brain biology and environment. One path of this reasoning, which is supposed to relieve us of the burden of our freedom to be evil, is the assumption that some people are just somehow born morally and ethically defective. Needless to say this creates a large controversy in the scientific and psychological community because it leads to a sort of genetic prejudice that consigns whole sets of people to the behavioral junk pile.

But don't be fooled. What is going on is exactly the same as we talked about earlier concerning embracing unhappiness to avoid being against ourselves, against our values, against what we are supposed to hold dear and adhere to. The public self punishing behaviors of sports stars, the feelings of shame and embarrassment we feel in so many different social contexts are as noted above, the tip of the iceberg in terms of how we use the pain of unhappiness as a tool for self-control. What we are learning is that we could know what we value and what we desire. No unhappiness in the form of making up a thing called "needs" or feeling the fear of failure or judgments is required to motivate us to go after what we want. We do not have to fear that unless we make what we want a matter of losing our happiness, we will not be serious in our intent to get what we want. When we return to the roots of our being, then our desires will be what they can be, a relaxed and enjoyable way of exploring the world.

EXPER/CISE

Over the course of several days, record how many times you place your happiness at risk by insisting that you "need" something in order to be okay with yourself. When you have accumulated a dozen or so instances, then spend some time reviewing each one and seeing whether it is really worth giving up your happiness if you should happen not to get this "need" fulfilled.

FREEDOM, THE HEART OF OUR JOY

> *Man came forth out of freedom and issues into freedom. Freedom is a primordial source and condition of existence....The mystery of the world abides in freedom....Freedom is at the beginning and at the end....Men, as Dostoevsky has shown with such amazing power, often renounce freedom to ease their lot.*
> **Nicolas Berdyaev,** *Dream and Reality*

So we come finally to freedom as the medium for expressing our happiness. We may want everything or nothing in the world. It does not matter since no particular desire or lack of a particular desire has any relevance for our happiness. That is strictly our business as we go about the Joywork of creating ourselves in ways we see fit. Of course we do this against the backdrop of the cultural world and its values and since nothing is required in order for us to be happy, we can live in comfortable consonance with the covenants of our culture, even when our preferences about how we would like things to be are in many cases limited by such a conformity. Again, the world does not always cooperate with our values, with our desires and wants. Yes, I know the preceding statements may not yet represent how you experience yourself right now. But, how wonderful it could be to come to know and experience that we are not diminished in our ability to experience our happiness because of what the world and society may present to us. In other words, we are **not** trapped in the "B" premise of the ABC's and therefore are **not** doomed to try and make the world conform to our wants so we can be happy. As the founder of Option noted: "We are the sole arbiters of our emotional states." Nothing can come between us and our freedom to take up a stance or attitude toward what is happening now this very instant.

REVIEW: Sections 6 through 8

6. From a review of the Option questions you began to learn how to untangle your unhappiness by seeing how we internally "twist" our arms to make ourselves conform to our own and others' expectations.

7. In this section we took up *belief* again and noted how this is the sole agent of our unhappiness. ***What we believe is what we feel.*** Then we looked at *Fear*, which is itself a ***belief that we are going to have unhappiness in the future and there is nothing we can do about it.*** So we instantly feel unhappy, in whatever form that will take, NOW!

Then we looked at a further development of fear which is ***dread.*** Here because we mistakenly get lost in the "B" assumption of the ABC's, we may include the ***whole of ourselves in the "world"*** and because of that assumption find ourselves believing that we are ***without freedom*** (a freedom that we are ambivalent about in any case since we don't yet accept "C") and therefore ***helpless before forces over which we have no control.*** These forces may "force" our acquiescence to "bad" or "evil" attitudes and behaviors and therefore we will lose our very souls as it were in this dreadful existential state from which there is no exit.

8. Here we began with defining how happiness is seen under many circumstances as an ***illegitimate way to be.*** Being happy will get you judged as woefully out of step with what is expected of you. The threat of consequences hangs over your head if you defy this vision. Thus being happy could be seen as ***depriving you of your happiness!***

Then the logical follow-through for that is that we are actually urged to ***cultivate our unhappiness as a good way to be.*** This is seen as helping to mold our behaviors and curb our desires.

Speaking of desires, we saw further that wanting becomes complicated by *escalating into what we call "needs."* We do this because we believe that happiness lies in the realm of "B" (controlling the world or at least our portion of it), and that the *measure of our happiness is the degree to which our wants ("needs") are satisfied.* But then we are hit with a paradox because we could turn our desires, wants, "needs" towards things that the world in its cultural traditions decides are "bad" or "evil" for us. So now we may find ourselves "needing" things that are out of bounds, but seemingly driven by those needs according to the fearful scenario described in Section 7 above.

But, in the end, we spoke about our *freedom* and the possibility that "C" of the ABC's could be true for you. *This would make you the determiner of meaning for yourself and free you of the determinism and constraints found in "B."*

Wow! A big bite to digest, just like after Aunt Rose has laid an eight course dinner on you and is still yelling "Mangia" ("eat" in Italian) at your prostrate body, stuffed to the point of near death with exquisite goodies. So take "five" so to speak, go back and get comfortable with the material before moving on, if you wish.

CHAPTER FOUR

MOTIVATION

I have suggested that unhappiness is merely the belief that we will have to be unhappy. We come to believe in our needs, which are ways of being that we must conform to in order to be happy. Then we fear not being able to fulfill these demands and therefore fear the inevitability of our unhappiness in the future, though we immediately feel unhappy because of our belief in our coming unhappiness. A concept intimately involved in much of this is *motivation*. Motivation is experienced as a feeling of determination or willingness to do the things we say are consistent with our values and to avoid the things that are inconsistent with those values. This is where unhappiness in the forms of fear, dread, anger, rage etc. enter in. We wonder if we will be motivated to be the way we are supposed to be. We fear not being afraid or unhappy because without that as a goad we fear we will not do the things necessary to be happy. Or we will not avoid the things that will make us unhappy. While thankfully not everyone starts out from experiencing what I call the *unbearable wrongness of being*, still that is the absolute zero point of dread that unhappy people are scrambling to avoid experiencing by using all the other maneuvers of unhappiness described in the following categories and in all the varieties of unhappiness we will consider. We will start with 9. *The Fear of Selfishness*. Then we will take up the important notions of 10. *Fear of Being 'Bad' For Ourselves*, followed by 11. *Doing the Best We Know to Do* and finally consider 12. *Time and Unhappiness*. These will be the final categories we will look at before taking up individual instances of unhappiness and then moving on to happiness. Hopefully what will emerge gradually for you is the true simplicity of this Joybuilding perspective. It derives from the notions described above about belief and an ignorance, therefore, of the whole of what I have been calling the **ABC's of unhappiness and happiness**. Getting stuck in "B" and not being able to get to "C" is at the root of all unhappiness. Keep that in mind as we go along and it will help to keep you oriented.

9. FEAR OF SELFISHNESS

We believe that to be for ourselves, in support of ourselves, is wrong, that is selfish. By this I mean that if we support ourselves, if we affirm our happiness in the face of all the chorus of voices in our world that tell us this is wrong in so many instances, then we will find ourselves losing the community of the world, of those we cherish. But, to rephrase an old saying, *if I am not for myself, then who shall be for me? If not now, then when?* How could being for ourselves be wrong? Only if doing so would lead to unhappiness as we have believed. That is what is so often reinforced by social/cultural norms. We fear being happy in certain instances when others would find our happiness inappropriate (they will many times take it to mean we don't care or are unmindful of the implications of events in the world, i.e., deaths, wars, natural disasters, sickness etc.). We believe that experiencing happiness would be "selfish" in such cases and by doing so would actually ultimately lead us to unhappiness when we lose the fellowship of others. However, the "ish" in selfish merely means relating to, or being a characteristic of a self!

On that basis, one could define all happiness as "selfish" because it relates to and indeed is a basic characteristic of the self.

What we fear is that by being *for* ourselves, we thereby will be *against* others, or against the ideals of the community, i.e., the greater good. **But the truth is that all are seeking their happiness and if they cannot experience it, then they seek to avoid the greater unhappiness.** This is absolute in all cases. There are no exceptions. In other words, if I can't get Aunt Rose to make me a gorgeous plate of eggplant capanota, I will settle for a slice of good bread and some olive oil. If a child cannot get some praise out of a parent, they may settle for at least not getting some criticism. In extreme cases, we may even surrender our very lives to save us from what we consider a greater distress, pain or some form of what we consider intractable unhappiness.

What then are the ideals of the community, this mysterious greater good, before which we are to yield our happiness and display unhappiness when demanded of us? Is not this greater good the fund of myths and covenants that have been formed in part at least out of human unhappiness and fear of the effects of happiness? So why would we listen to visions that have their roots partially in beliefs in necessary miseries? If we are called upon to hate our neighbor because he or she is of another race or religion or lifestyle, should we do so? If we are called upon to be unhappy about how our friends, family have failed to get some aspect of what they want out of their lives, including our cooperation in being some way they say we have to be in order for them to be happy, do we want to surrender our happiness in cooperation with that demand? That is what this Workbook will help you to decide. Remember, there is no call here for you to be without a loving regard for others. But does a loving regard have to be accompanied by unhappiness in whatever form demanded of us by others before they will recognize that loving regard as legitimate? This is the core of the issue of "selfishness."

Let us look at this from another perspective. Suppose we were to approach our common pragmatic problems out of our selfishness, that is, out of our being unafraid to affirm our happiness, then would that not be a more congenial atmosphere for humans to create solutions to those problems? How would that work?

Well let's go back to the *ABC's:*

> *A/ There is just you and the world*
> *B/ You don't control the world*
> *C/ You do control the attitude that you create in response to whatever the world presents to you at any given moment.*

What we have seen is that the major problems with how humans relate to themselves and others causes us to get stuck in "B." For so long as hope for happiness is seen to reside only in the realm of "B," then all of human striving will be to find better ways through technology and also through *ideologies* to dominate the world and bend it to our will. An ideology is the technology of believing that you have found the way to control the world of human behavior and relationships through some religious or political power/myth system. Now the operative mechanism for achieving this has been *power*, here defined as the ability to successfully manipulate some portion of the world and make it do our bidding. For both science (in modern times) and ideologues (throughout human history), this has often meant controlling people! And since very few humans have come close to accepting "C," then all the solutions have been worked out in terms of "B." Are you with me so far? Okay.

What that has meant in practical terms is exercising power to make other humans conform to some ideological scheme thought up by various people as the best way for people to live their lives. And if they disagree? Well, that's where power comes in. Because the one (or ones) with the power have been the ones capable of threatening other humans with the deprivation of the possibility of participating in any of the rewards of controlling the world even marginally. Thus, not to be obedient to the ideology (religion, political belief etc.) has often resulted in punishments. These punishments range from being deprived of physical comforts, access to food and shelter, positions in society, exile and ultimately the deprivation of liberty and life. ***Fear***, I think you will agree, has been the main ingredient in enforcing these views and we have a good understanding of what fear is from our work in Section 7, right? I don't have to catalogue the history of power and fear operating in human societies over time do I? Recent times and experiences with Nazism, Communism and revived religious fundamentalism that spawned 9/11 should jog your memory. And if you are interested in knowing more of my perspective on power, you can go to my *Unbearable Wrongness of Being* and pick up on my redoing of Dostoevsky's "Legend of the Grand Inquisitor" to see how power is found in what he terms "Miracle, Mystery and Authority."

So, how would embracing "C" improve matters? Well right from the get go, humans affirming "C" would not be driven by or intimidated by the ideologies and the power brokers manipulating those ideologies that are based completely on a "B" solution. Happiness would not reside in controlling the world. There would be no need to exercise power at all costs in the belief that you must control the world to have any happiness. Now that ***does not*** mean that humans would stop being interested in controlling as much of the world as their knowledge and technology might allow. Why not? After all, while we might understand that our happiness does not depend on that control, we could still very much want to create as much comfort and opportunity to explore the world as we possibly could. Now that is where coming from the perspective of "C" would encourage people to work together without the threat of the assumptions working in the ideologies of "B." Remember, those assumptions are that we do not control our attitudes and that we can be deprived of our happiness by the power of other individuals or of nature in some fashion. Isn't it true in your experience that when you are experiencing your joy, that you are much more relaxed and open to the perspectives of others, much more willing to be flexible because you are not feeling any kind of threat of fear working within you? Now that may be only of short duration in your life. Just imagine the result of doing your Joywork and increasing your ongoing sense of joy by many times. There is where you will begin to see the possibilities alive in living your joy, first for you and then for others who may share this perspective. Is this just another grand Utopian scheme for changing the world? No, not at all. People will come to know this or not as the case may be. We can speculate on how that might affect humans on a large scale, but this Joywork in *this* moment is a decision for *you.*

Alternatively, ask yourself this question: has working on the condition of being human from the perspective of being unhappy in all the guises unhappiness has taken (self effacement, need for power over others, need to destroy so-called enemies or cleanse the earth of the infidel, of other racial groups. the ruling classes, the non-righteous etc., etc.,) down through the ages brought the kind of conditions that humans have sought? Well, if your answer is what I think it is, then how could being for yourself be anything but the most enlightened way to be? If you like substitute the word self-*full*-ness for self-*ish*-ness and you may get a clearer picture of what is really going on here. So to review what we have said, what we are being told is that by being for ourselves, indulging in so-called selfishness, we are really somehow against our happiness, and therefore somehow actually against ourselves. This notion of being against ourselves segues nicely to the next fear we have about our motivation. But before that, let's do another exper/cise to increase our understanding around this issue.

EXPER/CISE

- Take a day in your life and become particularly aware of the ways in which you yourself, those around you and the messages that are implied in the information sources available to you, may all overtly or subtly be demanding you surrender your happiness in specific instances. Note how being a part of a society, family or corporation may come with a price tag of "necessary miseries" to be suffered to demonstrate your caring or loyalty. Record them and then at your leisure decide whether being "selfish" by affirming your right to your joy and happiness on an ongoing basis and in the face of these demands really goes against what *you* value for yourself.

- Take a copy of your daily newspaper. Note all the headlines and stories that have to do with problems rooted in the use of power, coercion and violence locally and around the world. Do the same with the other media, TV, radio, magazines etc. As you note all of the different ways in which people try to control others, ask yourself repeatedly: "Do I really believe that this is how I would want the world to be for me?" Then begin to see by using the Option Method questions whether you really have to be unhappy about what you learn about the world, even while you may want no part of how others use power to constrain and injure their fellow humans.

10. FEAR OF BEING BAD FOR OURSELVES

This is a fear right on the threshold of the "unbearable wrongness of being me" feeling that we dread so much. Here are all our fears of being crazy, unlovable, an eternal victim, an eternal victimizer, a phony, a fraud, totally and willfully neglectful of ourselves and our supposed best interests, a loser, a hopelessly lazy ingrate, a social pariah, a hateful, evil person, a schmuck who is the butt of everyone's jokes, a patsy who invites the derision and disdain of all, a mark for others to cheat and treat as the piece of lowlife garbage and human detritus that we are. Wow, how would you like that on your resumé? The description of our deficits can be endless, an abyss of dread and a cauldron of seething helplessness. Uh oh! That doesn't sound too good does it?

Again, let us turn to our "ABC's" to understand this fear. By now I'll bet you can guess where the problem lies, right? "A" is practically unassailable as a statement "There is just you and the world." No problem there. And as for "C," the preceding paragraph would simply make no sense if you were truly to know and affirm "C" i.e., "I do control the attitude that I construct toward whatever the world presents to me each moment of my existence." Yup, it is "B" that is the zone of moans once more, i.e., "I don't control the world."

Now let us refine a bit more the notion of the "world." Recall in Section 7 we talked about how if we include the very sense of *what it feels like to be me* experience as part of the world that then we literally are swallowed up by "B" of the ABC's. If you keep that point of conscious self-awareness that we call "me" separate from "B" you will find that precious moment of freedom to acknowledge your happiness is available to you. You know you exist *now* as you read this (we will discuss the concept of "now" and the "me" experience more in the section on "Time"). That is an undeniable fact, indeed it is the *only* absolutely undeniable fact that you can assert with full confidence. *All* other facts about the world have some level of uncertainty about them precisely because they are subject to the laws of physics, but *not* that fact that you exist and are aware of your existence! This has always been a controversial, hot topic for philosophers, and now for philosophers of science, down through human history. I take as my minimal point of departure that Consciousness is a foundational truth of Being, a definite part of what is, just like matter, gravity, motion etc., but not part of the material universe in the same way your leg or a chair is a part of the universe. So when I am talking about you, I am referring to an utterly unique experience whose intimate dimensions are known to you alone and whose attitudinal expression is completely under your control.

The *manifestation* of this unique "me" experience is however subject to the laws of the material universe, because our bodies are the incredibly complex vehicle for this expression. But the distinction is still there. After all, if you lose an arm to accident or disease, *you* are still around, right?

Take for example, the French author, Jean-Dominique Bauby, who suffered from a rare disease (locked-in syndrome) that deprived him of all ability to express himself save for the fluttering of his eyelids. We see that one can be reduced to practically zero functioning and still be a *self* capable of incredible artistic expression as witnessed in his final masterpiece, *The Diving Bell, And The Butterfly.*

Now in our bodily experience, as we have seen from earlier discussions, there are dimensions, autonomic functions, like the startle reflex, that we don't normally exert control over. Additionally, we experience signals from our body that we have appetites for food, for sex, that are part of the physiological package of who we are. Then, there are our beliefs or values deriving from our socialization with others, from which come our wants, or "needs" (as explained in Section 8). Now, while the *"things"* that we may want may be in the world and therefore not under our control, the *"wanting"* of them **is** under our control. What's the point? The point is that by clarifying what is truly in the realm of "B" and what is truly controlled by you, we can address the fear that describes the heading of this section, i.e., that we could be "bad for ourselves."

When people live with such intense doubts about their own self-worth and further feel tortured by what may seem like these mysterious feelings or "urges" in their bodies, they may try to devise strategies to "cover up" what is going on inside them. So for example we have the caricature of the bully's psychology: someone who picks on others and seeks power over them as a way to avoid revealing his/her own painful sense of being strange or inadequate.

But like all strategies built on unhappiness, there are serious flaws and weaknesses. We may still suspect others somehow have figured out what a schmuck we are despite our surface poses, and although we have many times no direct proof, we may think that they hold poor opinions of us or, more extremely, are actively spreading gossip about us or working against our personal interests somehow. This can escalate so that we may indeed live out the caricatures of others' expectations of us. Again, at least the way we assume they see us, because we often assume "as if" states in deciding what other people's feelings for us really are. That is, we feel unhappy "as if" something had occurred, that could make us unhappy whether we know it has occurred for sure or not. For example, we may believe that someone has cheated us or said things behind our back and this may in reality not be the case. But we act **as if** it were and feel unhappy according to our beliefs about such a matter. Thus we can create ourselves to be the "monsters" that we fear we are and end up in some destructive, even aggressive posture in relation to others or to society in general. We do so on the grounds of being absolutely enraged that others have seen us so clearly to be what we fear we are. Now we may believe we must live in the light of that public exposure and humiliation. As I describe this at the end of my book *Joywords,* the logic of such thinking can produce such pain that we may spiral down to incredibly bizarre dead ends of dread and hatred.

At the core is a belief in the presence within us of some kind of innate self defeating, self destructive "urges", urges that somehow have the ability to overwhelm any other desire we have to attain happiness, urges before which we are helpless and can only wait for the assumed dreaded outcomes to happen. Let us look a bit closer at this notion of "urge" both from the perspective of its physiological roots and its sociocultural manifestations. As noted above, the logic of the "B" assumption of the ABC's will apply.

What we do have are the experiences of our physiology with its startle reflex potentials and with its appetites for the maintenance of existence (food, eating, possibly some kind of physical contact/stimulation at a very early age, shelter, safe environment) and the perpetuation of the species (sex).

In addition to that basic physiological layer, we create (often in concert with and as an extension of that basic layer) a series of what we call "needs"(as per Section 8 *The Dread of Not Getting What We Want*) based on the need to control notion of "B" of the ABC's. Thus an "urge" is simply a stronger form of what we term a "need" but seen much more on the order of something over which we have limited or even no control. "Urges," "impulses," understood in this light, follow from the logic of "B" and the notion of "need" as something necessary to our existence in order for us to be happy. They are beliefs, just like "needs," that we have about ourselves or the world. Now, it is of course true that in the natural order of things our physical feelings, appetites, may press for recognition in our awareness, but they can never force us into a behavior that we do not wish. All the *intensity* of "urges" therefore ***are self-created out of the assumptions alive in our beliefs.***

The distinction may be seen as follows: I may say I have a "need" to eat, but then I may also say I have this uncontrolled urge to leap into a pan of Aunt Rose's lasagna and inhale the entire batch. You see, once I have posited a thing called a "need," now there is a pressure coming from my beliefs that will possibly envelop the whole process of eating with unnecessary conflict. Sure, I feel a thing called appetite which lets me know that my body requires nourishment if I want it to thrive. I can be comfortable with that and enjoy my physiological makeup, or I can complicate it by calling my appetite a "need" and now begin to worry about food instead of seeing it as an area of pleasurable opportunity in the world to cooperate with the natural momentum of my body. That sense of conflict about food can be turned into an uncomfortable, and for some frightening, thing called an "urge."

The problem is that if we stick ourselves with this logic in the realm of "B" we soon run into a wall of conflict between our "needs" now seen in some cases as "urges" and the structure of the authorized permission giving dictums of a given society or culture. For their own ends, societies/cultures generally support the notion of "needs," (need to defend your nation, need to be a good citizen, need to be faithful to values of family and hard work, as defined by the individual culture; need to observe laws, covenants, contracts etc.). However, they will be wary of the "urges" that arise in many cases as unwelcome side effects of the "needs" concept. So for example, they will support the "need" to procreate, keep the marriage bond intact and produce citizens, BUT, it will lay down moral imperatives in varying degrees of severity, depending upon the cultural belief system, **against sexual urges**!

Let me illustrate. Not too long ago I was watching a program on the Middle East and at one point a Muslim cleric of some great stature was shown speaking to a group of men. What he was explaining to them was why women had to dress in the *burkha* a garment that literally enshrouds them from head to feet, so that only the eyes and nose are allowed to show (we have all become acquainted with them through the confining dress codes that obtained for women under the Taliban). His reasoning was simple. You (the men he was speaking to) are fallen creatures and totally incapable of controlling your sexual urges. Therefore, in the interests of public order and religious commitment to ordered family life, women must don these ponderous robes because were they to expose the slightest part of their bodies, ***they would incite you beyond your ability to control yourselves and thus lead you into sin!*** Recall again images of women being beaten by the keepers of the moral order because they exposed some part of their body.

You see, just as with the distrust of desire you find in the Hindu/Buddhist tradition, you find a basic distrust (called original sin in the Christian tradition) of "urges" in the Judeo-Christian-Islamic traditions. Thus the emphasis on control through systems of internalized imperatives called moral values.

Now I think it is clear that one of the main functions that a culture takes upon itself according to its beliefs, is to protect you from your "urges," that is to protect you from yourself! The ideal is to channel the urges into acceptable cultural pathways (like marriage, commerce, politics, religion, competition, even war, etc.) and so to make them dovetail with the "needs" created by that culture to sustain its own interests.

Often the "urges" are demonized as pathways through which "evil" enters the world, because "evil" is associated with all those things we do not control according again to the logic of "B." Therefore, those entities which are seen to "provoke" "urges" are also viewed with suspicion and prejudice. Women have taken a lot of abuse from men because as noted in the earlier anecdote, they are seen as the source of temptation. Right from Eve, through the myths of the siren, succubae, witches, etc., women have been persecuted and constrained by this belief in "urges" and forced into manners of dress, living (the tradition of the harem) and behaving . In certain parts of the world, Brazil for example, men are literally free to kill their wives if they believe them to be unfaithful, because the logic of "B" says that they have no control over their emotions when faced with such an "enormous affront" to their macho sensibilities [this is to say there will be no practical legal penalty, though this is happily changing]! Thus we can see how powerful this fear of our "self destructive urges" is. Again the executions of women under the Taliban were regular events.

But there is a grand flaw in this fear all based, again, on the "need to control in order to be happy," hypothesis derived from "B" of the ABC's. "Urges" are an artifact of that "need" hypothesis, a self created intensification of basic physiological appetites and inclinations that is rooted in fear and dread. But, since we fear them, often with enormous intensity, it stands to reason we are using our fear as we always use our fear, that is to either motivate us to do or to avoid something. Remember, all we do no matter what is done to avoid feeling bad! The only reason we are afraid of our "urges" is because we are afraid we will desire them and that will ultimately lead to more unhappiness. In this case our fear, however useless it may actually be in helping to achieve happiness, clearly demonstrates that we really want our happiness and find what we call our "urges" to be something alien to that effort.

If we start with unhappiness and then try to use unhappiness to remedy our unhappiness, the result will always be the same, that is, unhappiness, sometimes in greater intensities than we began with!

All kinds of so-called pathological states are derived from following the twisted logic of mistrusting ourselves and our legitimate right to be happy. The right to be happy is the **only** actual right we possess because it is the only state of being over which we have total control. All other so-called rights are contingent upon the historical, socio-political context in which we find ourselves. *You* have rights only to the degree that *others* mutually recognize and respect them. Your control over that is subject to change as circumstances for humans clearly show. You **do always** have a right to attempt to get others to acknowledge your rights to possess and dispose of political and material goods and services, but **only** in the case of happiness is your right absolute. And that is because your happiness is not contingent on anything or anyone else but **your** own freedom and willingness to affirm your happiness in any given moment.

What we can see, then, is that so much unhappiness that is described in psychological terms falls under this heading of believing that there is something wrong with us. Now, as mentioned earlier, we try to keep ourselves in control by internalizing checks and balances, which are really threats to ourselves that we will feel unhappy in some form if we do not comply with those internalized values. Thus we use the pain or the threat of emotional distress to try to maintain some sort of stability. But the strategies of maintaining allegiance to those values often create distress of varying intensities in ourselves over the possibility that we might lapse in our vigilance. Living in those states of unhappiness becomes unbearable at times, so we seek some sort of relief in experiencing good feelings. Cultures know this and provide escape valves of sorts by allowing members of a society to engage in activities that encourage some fun and relaxation. So religious and political festivals, family gatherings etc. often provide a chance for indulging in some welcome distraction from maintaining that internal vigilance. Dancing, singing, eating together, often according to age old traditions approved by the society, are universal forms of letting off steam. In more loosely ruled, democratic societies, our options are much broader and less defined by tradition. But what it all amounts to is the occasional allowing of good or pleasurable feelings through what I call ***permission giving devices***. That means that we will only allow ourselves to feel pleasurable, "good" feelings when we have fulfilled some behavioral ritual or act that we have designated, sometimes in accordance with the general prescriptive norms of a culture or society, sometimes more aside from or in direct contradiction to those norms based on our own idiosyncratic belief system.

I call that assemblage of beliefs at the heart either of a cultural/ideological perspective or in the actual living base of assumptions and beliefs in any individual the ***iconic core***. These are the rules and permission giving devices that regulate access to equanimity for the social structure and of course are realized in the individual to the extent that that individual adheres to those strictures in their moment to moment existence. Some may internalize very restrictive versions and stay closely within the lines permitted by that version, others simply don't require of themselves as strict a translation. Their iconic core index is lower simply because they allow that to be that way for themselves. This is the wonder of being human; so many retain an inner profile of greater joy even while giving lip service by their outward behavior and demeanor to the iconic core's demands. Even in carrying out the requirements of the strictest ideologies, we individualize our responses through our freedom. This represents a vast reservoir of joy and felicity that lives as a silent hidden ocean beneath the surface crusts of conformity and restraint waiting to be tapped by the hope a more compassionate perspective might offer them.

This is where the problem with our theme in this section, *Being Bad for Ourselves* comes in. If we are acting out of permission giving devices that are fully within the acceptable norms, then most times there will be no problem. However, because the interpretation of what is best for us, and how we should properly live our lives is so varied, we in so many instances will deviate a little or a lot from the acceptable norms and provide our-selves with permission giving devices that are in conflict with our internalized values and beliefs. So, what we get, then, is an endless cycle beginning with feeling constrained by our values and living out some anxiety, longing, sense of lack or inadequacy, anger, frustration, failure, guilt etc. as a means of maintaining those internal values and that external stability. Then we reach a point where we override those internal values and their accompanying unhappy feelings that guard and maintain them. We allow our permission giving devices to kick in and act out the behaviors that are the expression of those devices. We smoke even though we "know" it is "bad" for us. We overeat, even though we "know" it is "bad" for us. We drink or take drugs; we have sexual encounters in contradiction to our values; we indulge in power operations or "trips" to give ourselves a sense of exhilaration in denigrating, judging or even physically abusing or, in the extreme, even killing others.

Let us take a look at some diagrams of how this works that might make it clearer. I call this the paradoxical unhappiness loop.

THE UNHAPPINESS LOOP

All unhappiness is locked in a cycle that turns back on itself. That is because it follows the logic of "B" of the "ABC's" which requires control of the world in order to be happy. Since control of the world is always subject to the uncertainty of the laws of physics and the mind set and beliefs of others, there is no sure way we can maintain such control. In this scenario, our starting point is some attempt to maintain a conformity with what we think our values should be. When this attempt strains our capacity to maintain it, we seek relief through permission giving devices as described here in this depiction

The initial state of unhappiness which we use to motivate , control and manipulate our behavior becomes too painful and constraining so that we

6. We try to reduce the dread by reconstituting the control that we believed our original state of misery afforded us. Thus we punish ourselves for allowing this permission giving behavior to occur and we there by attempt to teach ourselves to refrain from such behavior in the future. To do this we return to some version of "1."

2. seek relief in the allowing of some good feelings, at first, perhaps, within the constraints we have created in co- operation with the values/beliefs we have adopted in the course of our lives (permission giving devices). If this proves insufficient for relief, then we may follow a need driven path and exceed social norms, a little or a lot.

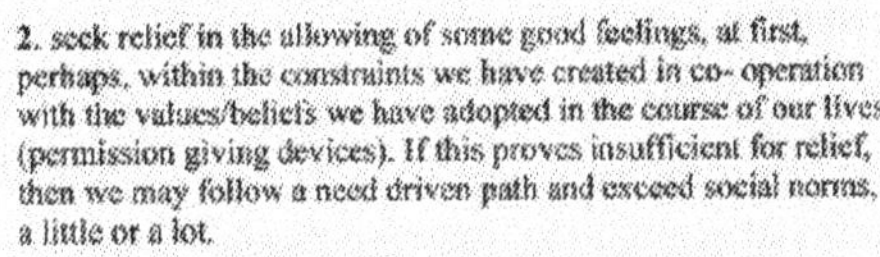

3.The behavior which allows the good feelings is acted out---ranging from anything as innocuous as having a cigarette, a glass of wine, watching a sitcom, to "pigging out" on Aunt Rose's lasagna, feeling driven to have sex or drugs or perpetrate violence on others out of a "need" or "urge" to experience power in order to give yourself permission internally to feel good!

5. Now we feel regret, remorse, guilt, disgust etc.. at having indulged in the behavior and a counter, paradoxical reaction of dread begins to set in.

4.The good feelings are temporarily felt. But the permission giving device begins to dissolve because the contexts change, the behaviors are self-limiting (you are stuffed, the drug wears off, the sex is over, the victim is subdued or dead!)

It simply repeats itself, as you see, without any resolution. Why? Because as long as you stay within the logic of "B" of the ABC's, there is no resolution. (Check at the end of Section 7 for a review and recall what we said a page or so earlier about how the use of unhappiness to solve the problems of unhappiness can only result in more unhappiness). This loop actually applies to all forms of unhappiness. Now some will object that there are categories of people, called psychopaths, who are living proof of what happens when you care only for your own happiness. These people are dreaded precisely because they seem to fit a caricature of the totally amoral, totally unfettered individual who out of that alleged freedom and happiness decides to perpetrate "evil" on his fellows. The character Hannibal Lecter in the movie "Silence of the Lambs," and later "Hannibal" played with such panache by Anthony Hopkins, epitomizes this fear we have of our happiness.

That is why movies about serial killers are so popular of late, precisely because they capture the public's image of happiness gone amok and reinforce the necessity for "*healthy misery*" to preserve us and others from the disastrous effects of such insane felicity. But are such people as described in fiction really compatible with the way people act in real life? I would assert they are not. The case histories of so called psychopaths are replete with descriptions of how enraged they were and how those intense feelings of unhappiness manifested in their savagery towards their victims. No, it is not happiness that so called psychopaths achieve with their violent, destructive acts, but rather a release of the enormous internal tensions of unhappiness that they carry as a belief package with them into their daily lives. The acts give them some temporary remission from that pain and some temporary permission to feel a glimmer of contentment.

But remember, the logic driving the "psychopath," is the same as that driving the ideologue, the righteous and the terrorist. It is exclusively "B" logic from the ABC's. Let me illustrate by some items that are newsworthy at the time I am writing this paragraph. First, a manhunt that gripped the country for weeks came to an abrupt end with the discovery of the suicide of Andrew Cunanan, the murderer of the designer Versace, along with lesser known individuals. In an interview done with one of Cunanan's roommates of some years, it was disclosed that he (Cunanan) was obsessed with self-image and power and never felt comfortable except when he actually held or was under the illusion that he held, power over others. His tastes in sex ran more and more radically to sadistic practices of inflicting pain on others. His roommate theorized that he killed Versace out of a pique of jealousy that while he (Cunanan) was becoming a "nobody" going "nowhere" in his life, Versace was the epitome of the gay man with enormous power and prestige; a vision of everything Cunanan wanted (in order to feel happy, of course) but felt he could never achieve. Thus he killed the icon of his ideal person, but actually was trying to kill the "unbearable wrongness of being" in himself that flooded him with feelings of being so "bad" and unworthy that only a steady diet of permission giving devices based on power would allow some relief. However, the behavioral rituals that would provide the relief grew in intensity from merely whipping to actually torturing and murdering others. It culminated in Versace, after which the inexorable logic of "B" led Cunanan to put a bullet in his own brain to kill the pain.

Another incident, this time in Kobe, Japan is even more to the point. I will quote a section from the *New York Times* of Sunday, June 29, 1997:

> The police announced tonight that they had arrested a 14-year-old boy who, they said, had confessed to the beheading last month of an 11-year-old boy, the grisliest murder in the memory of Japan.
>
> The arrest of the ninth grader, a neighbor and acquaintance of the victim, stunned the Japanese and is certain to add to worries that many young people have lost their moral bearings. The police did not identify the suspect, who lives in the western city of Kobe, or say much about him or his family.

The killing of the 11-year-old, Jun Hase, has transfixed Japan in part because of its savagery: his head was left resting on the front gate of a junior high school, with a defiant message stuffed in the mouth. Just as horrifying, the killer went out of his way to taunt the police and threaten more slayings.

"I can relieve myself of hatred and feel at peace only when I'm killing someone," the killer said in a letter sent to a local newspaper. *"I can ease my pain only by seeing others in pain."* (Italics mine.)

Now, you can see from this news item that a whole society is rocked by the apparent failure of their internalized control devices (shame, loss of "face" and honor are the chief methods of maintaining order in Japanese society and have done so splendidly in the opinion of many) to ward off the activities of this young man. Dread rises up in them and in many of us over the existence of such people. But, are they the real danger to us?

Cultures, including our own, have pinned their hopes on the internalization of such pain giving experiences as guilt, shame, embarrassment etc., to ward off the demons of uncontrolled "urges." Yet, I hope you have begun to see that these urges are themselves the products of the very methods designed to ward them off!

Let's look at another news item that will help make the point here. It describes the activity, not of psychopaths but of dedicated fundamentalists who were out to change the face of culture and society and rid it of the kinds of problems represented by an Andrew Cunanan or the unnamed murderer described by the *Times* piece. Here in a news item from that same paper dated Sunday, July 20, 1997, is an excerpt from a manual for interrogators/torturers put together by the Cambodian Khmer Rouge Communist fundamentalist regime of Pol Pot. I quote from one section and the bold italics are mine:

Elaborating on the aims of torture, the manual condones killing even as it cautions against it:

The purpose of torture is to get (prisoners') confessions. *It is not something we do for the fun of it.* Thus we must make them hurt so that they respond quickly. Another purpose is to break them and make them lose their will. *It's not something done out of individual anger or for self satisfaction.* Thus we beat them to make them afraid absolutely not to kill them. When torturing it is necessary to examine the prisoners' state of health first and necessary to examine the whip.

Don't try to quickly kill them—bring them to death.

Now, do you see what I am getting at here? Note the difference. Whereas the "psychopath" is operating out of his/her own idiosyncratic system of beliefs and aiming at using the rituals of violence and murder to gain some relief, the fundamentalist ideologues are torturing for their own religious/political/societal purposes. They want to control the process, and they precisely forbid their torturers to use this as a means of gaining any unauthorized pleasure from what they do! For example, the Commandant of Auschwitz noted at his trial that he allowed no gratuitous cruelty in the extermination of the Jews! In fact, those torturers caught using the process in this way were subject to severe penalties themselves as this news item from the same article points out pungently (italics are mine):

Another interrogator was arrested in 1978 *for doing his job with too much enthusiasm.* This is from his confession:

After questioning (suspected subversives) one morning, one created an incident jumping off the third story. Then he hurled his head against something and broke it open. As soon as I took him back where he belonged, I called over Chhay and Teng to help me beat him. At that time we beat him to death. I didn't report the death immediately. I waited in order to throw the upper echelons off the track *so they wouldn't notice that I had slipped up and snuffed him immediately.*

One has only to recall the diaries and letters of the 9/11 fanatics to see again how they were guided by rigid, religious prescriptions in the carrying out of their mission. I think it fair to say then, the greatest destruction to humans over the centuries has been wrought not by soulless psychopaths who have lost their moral boundaries and are drunk on unauthorized bouts of happiness and joy, but rather precisely by men of conscience who were acting righteously out of their beliefs and often described great misgivings about the carnage they felt they had to produce to achieve their ends. Religious, political, ideological belief systems often helped to assuage their sorrows by affirming that it was correct (The Jews are an 'evil' race; the bourgeoisie and the nobility must be destroyed to open the doors for the proletariat; the infidel must be annihilated etc.) and it was their duty to kill or subdue the non-believer, the racially impure, the class enemy. One could say that this ideological belief provided that helpful sense of being congruent with what you do. By doing the behaviors (the killing, torturing etc.), you are affirming the "righteousness" of your beliefs. So conscience does not make cowards of us all as Shakespeare has Hamlet complain early in that play. Indeed, Hamlet manages to put away his share of bodies before it is all over. But, keeping the psychopath out front in the public mind serves the culture well as a dire warning to those who would give free rein to their right to happiness. Because, in summary, once we have allowed ourselves to believe in a thing called "urges" then *what we dread the most is not dreading our urges!*

EXPER/CISE

- Examine the methods of self-control you have used during your life to cope with whatever you might describe as "impulses" or "urges." This could have been (or be) around food, or sex, or ambitions of some sort. With food, can you be in touch with how possibly your sense of "craving" may come from a sense of "needing" to eat? That is, you have lost the comfort of wanting to eat and treat it out of some acquired tradition of discomfort based on your experience growing up. Now of course, as we noted there are physiological factors at work that influence how our body responds, but even with those involved, notice how your unhappiness can diminish as you clear up beliefs around these issues. More is to come so just play with what you can learn at this point and move on.

11. DOING THE BEST WE KNOW TO DO

This is another key concept flowing out of the understanding of ourselves as free and as choosing in each moment what we think is appropriate based on what we believe. How can we do anything else except make the best choices we know to make at each and every turn of our lives? Now, based upon what we have come to understand about how we come to believe in the value of unhappiness, we can understand that those beliefs colored how we came to choose whatever we chose. After the fact of having chosen whatever we chose, whether it be years after or only an instant after, we might immediately alter our vision of what we value and know that what we just chose to do now no longer represents what we want for ourselves. In other words, just as we will see in our discussion of time, we may come to another moment in our lives when we can make another choice and that choice does not have to be prejudiced by our past choices, no matter what their practical consequences may have been.

Look, recall earlier in the first Exper/cise, you were asked to do the "Aunt Rose" stories from your past, incidents that had emotional charge years ago, but held no such feelings for you now. You were making decisions about what was important to you then: your red bike which your sister broke, your missed opportunity to sleep over with the other guys because your parents thought you were still too young, the speeding ticket you got just two weeks after you got your license, the hubcaps you stole in a little experimenting with petty crime, the marijuana or coke you used so that you wouldn't be thought of as a wimp, etc., etc. The list is almost endless. As you reflect on the vast ribbon of memories of behaviors that now are either silly or antithetical to your values at present, what is there to say? Some of those incidents had little or no practical impact; others may have proved minor or severe impediments to your desires to prosper in this world. But at each and every instant when you were in those now vanished moments, you were acting on your beliefs. From the vantage point of this moment, now, when you are reflecting upon these activities, you may indeed have other perspectives that would color your choices. But that is totally irrelevant to what is past, **precisely because it is past**, that is to say it does not exist as a real moment in which action can be taken!

Thus there is no place for regret, or guilt understood as being unhappy about our past choices in order *through that unhappiness* somehow to restore our right to be happy again. You see, it is the same old thing: let's give ourselves a dose of unhappiness now over what we did moments or years ago. This will act as a prophylactic to prevent us from being a way we don't want to be in the future. Others often attempt to impress on us the need for guilt by specific punishments.

But, really, we can know that we value now what we value now, even if it's completely different from what we may have valued an instant or years ago. We don't need the pain of guilt or regret to prompt or motivate us to know what we know. Now the world may dole out consequences for our actions if those actions violate the covenants of our society. But those violations will come many times out of our believing in some form of unhappiness that makes us feel obsessed or compelled to behave in ways that may even become extreme in the pursuit of what we have come to believe we somehow "need" for our happiness. This is just a repetition of what we described in the previous section as "permission giving devices" that sometimes conform to the ideals of culture and society about what fits the definition of a need and sometimes become some idiosyncratic dread driven drive that may be radically out of synch with the ideals of society. The examples I gave will hopefully still be alive in your memory.

Okay, what we could know from the perspective of our joy now is that we do not have to knowingly violate the rules of society and jeopardize our physical freedom and safety out of believing in anything called a "need" or "urge" that is required for our happiness. But if in our lives we have done things that, **now** out of a **new** understanding of ourselves, we no longer would in any way want or desire to do, we could know that without emotional pain of any kind. By now I presume you are not stealing hubcaps, or tossing firecrackers on poor old Mrs. Thistlewood's decrepit porch on the fourth of July, or getting in a rage when your sister gets to watch her "stupid" program on TV instead of yours. However, you may indeed be getting unhappy over whatever it is that your present values and beliefs prompt you to be unhappy about. It may no longer be about bicycles, firecrackers, and TV programs, but bank accounts, marriages, children and careers. So be it. You are now learning your "ABC's," so as you go through your Joywork, this may change for you. Whatever you have done, however you have been: that represents everything up to this moment. If there have been consequences, if others have been compromised or truly hurt by your behavior, then are you not in a much better position to redress those consequences when you are coming from your joy, rather than from your sorrow? Is it not conceivable that you can conjure up much more enthusiasm for mending the broken pieces of the past with the outlook of "C" of the ABC's rather than the twisted braids of pain generated by the logic of "B"?

In summary, if we had truly known to do differently, then we would have done so. But we **truly believed** whatever we did believe at the **instant** we acted. So, while we are **responsible** for our actions, and may be subject to consequences, we are not to **blame** in the sense that our actions can make us "bad" or "evil." Being responsible is affirming the truth about a cause and effect relationship and assigning consequences according to our covenants and laws. Blame is a requirement to be unhappy about our own or others' actions in order to demonstrate that we disapprove of them. The point is that we could realize that we do not have to relinquish our happiness because of our past. Aunt Rose used to say that you can't season last week's tomato sauce this week. You can only make sure that what goes in the pot is what you truly want now. ***Nothing can destroy our access to our happiness except our decision to deny it to ourselves****!*

EXER/CISE

- I am going to count to three and when I reach three I want you right now to do something that *you do not want to do!* Now, are you with me on this? Take your time and think of something that you do not want to do…….Okay? Do you have it? Here goes, ready? *One………Two………Threeeeeeeee! Boooooom*! You did it, right? Yes? No? What happened? What's that you say, you did do it, but you really didn't want to do it? Well then who did it? What? Yes. That's right. You did it! How did you do it? What? You say I told you to do it! Well I did ask you to do something, but you chose what to do, right? So ***you*** did it. Okay, you agree. But what's that? You say you didn't want to do it? Well how did it get done? Oh, again, you're telling me that I told you to do it. Come on, now. I made a request and you did it, right? ***Why?*** Oh, you really didn't want to do it, but you wanted to cooperate with me and please me so you did it, is that it? Hmmmm. So you are telling me that your reason for wanting to do what you say you did not want to do was because you are a nice person and you want to succeed at this Joybuilding Joywork. Ahhhh! Okay. So now you just told me ***why you wanted to do it!*** Okay? Do you get the point here? Whenever you do whatever you do, it is because you have a reason to do it; even while you complain about doing it, there is still you doing it for your own reasons, right? So in the moment you act, you act for the reasons you act. Now in this moment, you can decide that action was against what you now value or you can congratulate yourself for your perseverance. The comfort is that you are always doing what you want and you can always change your mind.

12. TIME AND UNHAPPINESS

Here is a good place to speak of our experience of time and unhappiness. We use a mental sleight of hand to skew our concept of time to produce a feeling of duration, that is a sense of the ongoingness or flow of our experience coming out of what we call the past, flitting by a fuzzily defined present and moving more nebulously and hypothetically into what we call the future. We do this by acting as if the last moment still exists and can somehow be accessed and that the future is somehow alive with its potentials in the present moment. What comes to mind is an old radio show that was essentially about the times and foibles of a Jewish immigrant family. One of the members of that family, an Aunt Rose type, who had not mastered English too well, used to get a lot of laughs with her mixing up of words and tenses. I distinctly remember her response to a question about a neighbor's whereabouts to have been " Oi, Rosalie, well *she moved tomorrow!"*

That funny mixture of the past and the future always stuck with me over the years because it seemed to capture our actual sense of time. We act as if we live not only in the present but somehow also in the recent past and the near future. That is a convenient way of operating in this world because it creates continuities and points of reference that allow us to move with ease and comfort through time and space. But, one of the byproducts of that skewing is a distortion by which we can increase our anticipatory dread. We do this by not attending to the truth about time, that is that we live and have our being only in the present! Go ahead, just try and munch **now** on Aunt Rose's crostini with roasted peppers that she is not going to make until **tomorrow**. Besides getting that special look from her accompanied by the *pazzo* hit on the side of her head and then the fingers extended in your direction, you will be chewing on empty air. There is no other time than right now, and that aperture of "nowness' is about one half second in duration. That is when things actually happen. *All other experience of time is what we carry along with us as information in the present about how things proceeded before this moment or hypotheses about what will happen after this moment.* That is the past and the future. Anything that is actually not now has no ability to affect us in the present. If a bullet just whizzed by our heads, then no matter what the potential it may have had as it was heading our way, the fact is that it no longer holds that potential because the laws of the material universe are operating on it and its trajectory hasn't any relevance for our safety any longer.

However, we can respond to the information as if it has relevance. And, indeed it might in some pragmatic sense, i.e. someone may be shooting at us and we can reasonably assume that they may send more bullets our way. However, in terms of beliefs/feelings, the startling dose of adrenalized awareness presented to us by our sensory system can be transformed into an anticipatory dread that we can maintain in our bodies long after the bullet or any practical peril may have passed. In other words we can take the information about the event, which was brief and no longer causally relevant in a material way, and make it the occasion for ongoing feelings of discomfort which occupy hundreds or thousands of those half second apertures known as the present. Thus we give a sense of duration to our miseries and lose contact with the unprejudiced opportunities that each present moment presents. In our minds we have created an ongoing duration of anxiety which we mistakenly attribute to the incident with the bullet, but which actually refers to our ANTICIPATION that terrible things will happen to us and most importantly that we have no control over how we will feel about those things! That sense of present unhappiness that we have created in response to the expectation that worse things are to come is the proof that we give ourselves that there will come a time when we will have to feel unhappy, even more dreadfully unhappy in the future, and we are helpless to alter that emotionally painful scenario.

So you can see how liberating it is to understand the truth about time. What is that truth? That each successive present moment is available for you to feel your joy and happiness no matter what the last moment may have brought and no matter what any future moments might bring. *The only time for you to feel anything at all is right now.* The only question is how do you want to feel right now? *No information that exists within your memory now has the power to deprive you of your bliss, no matter what it is.* You alone have the power to decide what your attitude is going to be toward whatever each moment presents to you, toward whatever information may reside in you as a past experience. This is the blessed logic and truth, as I see it, of "C" of the ABC's.

Still, whatever the facts may have been, any unhappiness is merely your interpretive response to whatever occurred. The fact that, based on your acculturation and beliefs, you have always responded in such and such a manner in the past in no way means that therefore you **must** respond in the same way in any **new** moment of your life. It only seems that way because of the experience of duration described above. No, now is completely free for you to make up a new way of being. You just don't believe that at this moment. I am going to help you to see things as they are and seize the moment for your joy and happiness. Rapture awaits you, but remember the words "rape" and "rapture" have the same root in the Latin *raptus, to seize.* It is just a matter of how you see the world. *Rape* is strictly a product of "B" logic, because it doesn't allow for freedom, it can't wait for a free response, but must "seize" what it wants in order to satisfy its "needs" and "urges." But *rapture*, now that is a different story; here you are not in the realm of "B" because rapture is a product of freedom and strictly a "C" phenomenon. *It is you seizing yourself with the awe of your own being and that of the world around you.*

EXPER/CISE

- Go to a private quiet place in the woods, by a lake or the sea or any-where that gives that sort of equivalent feel for you. Take a bunch of small pebbles or stones with you. Take them one by one, and stand-ing up with your hand about chest height, eyes closed, drop each one on to the ground or better yet, if you can arrange it, into the water. That is simply because you are likely to hear their impact more easily. Now it will take about a second for the stone to fall from chest height to the surface. That is just a bit longer than what the actual present seems to be according to cognitive researchers who conclude that the minimum time available to us for awareness is about one half a second. The Russian writer Dostoevsky in several of his novels alludes to the tale of how in the time it took for a drop of water to fall from Mohammed's pitcher to the ground, God showed him all the mansions of paradise. So, that tiny interval of "now" holds a lot for you to explore.

- Initially, allow about thirty seconds to pass between the dropping of each stone. See the degree to which you can become totally present with yourself in that one second it takes for the stone to fall from your hand to the surface. Then allow yourself to simply be with the afterglow of that awareness until you release the next stone and so on. After a bit, you can decrease the intervals from thirty to fifteen seconds. Gradually, you will decrease the intervals between drops, and you will increase your ease at being with yourself in the one sec-ond interval until you hear the tiny splash or sound of the stone hit-ting the ground. That sense of presentness will eventually provide you with an occasion for intensifying your joy. You will realize that "now" is an open canvass for you to color with the palette of your good feelings and you will have a ready reference point for instantly orienting yourself to be in the "now" even when you don't have a bunch of stones and a quiet environment available to you.

SUMMARY/Review

9. We learned that selfishness is made into a negative concept because in the "B" hypothesis where everybody is competing for control, culture and societies feel they must rein in the individuals' attempts at control. Otherwise the cohesiveness and power of the society will be destroyed in the rush of individuals to gain power over their fellows and their environment. Thus people are led to believe they must feel bad about their individual desires if those desires are not in synchrony with the larger purposes of a particular culture or social grouping. But we have seen in our own lives and in history the track record of feeling bad about ourselves to keep us in the moral framework of a culture.

10. In an allied theme, we explored the fear of being bad for ourselves and its roots again in the logic of the "B" hypothesis, that we must control the world in order to be happy. By including all of who we are in the realm of "B" we lose our freedom and individuality. Also, we assume that the world has the power to make us feel ways we don't want to feel against our will, or fear to feel, even though they can be attractive feelings. The concept of "urges" derives from this perspective and we find ourselves caught between the authorized "needs" supported by society, and our individual unauthorized "urges" that go beyond the bounds of the allowable. We also saw how "urges" are a mixing of our natural inclinations harnessed to the unhappy engine of our dreaded unauthorized "needs" to express ourselves and find some relief from the straightjacket of our cultural belief systems. We diagrammed this in the "unhappiness loop." Then we explored the myths of the psychopath and illustrated the truth about where the danger lies for us: not in the unauthorized expression of our joy, but in the ideological attempts to control the world and mold it into some parochial vision of how things have to be in order for us to be "good"(that is happy).

11. Here we learned that we are free to feel happy now no matter what our past actions have been. Whatever the consequences, we did what we knew to do in a particular moment and are now free to change our vision in this one.

12. In a connecting section on Time, we learned that we confuse the truth about time by making it something it is not, i.e., a duration of a past and future. By knowing that we only have now to be any way at all, we can liberate ourselves from being chained to the myths of the past or the dreaded expectations of the future. We can embrace our freedom and seize the moment to be now how we wish to be and live our joy from moment to moment.

CHAPTER FIVE

CATEGORIES OF UNHAPPINESS

UNHAPPINESS

THE FRUIT OF OUR MISERIES: UNTANGLING THE WEB

"The world is but a broken toy,
Its pleasures hollow, false its joy,
Its pains alone are true, Alas!
Its pains alone are true."
"Princess Ida" of Gilbert and Sullivan

CATEGORIES OF UNHAPPINESS

That little ditty of Gilbert and Sullivan certainly does sum up the "B" world of the ABC's. It is what we so often come to when our attempts to gain control in order to be happy are frustrated by the world's lack of cooperation with our wants. In this section we will take categories of unhappiness and briefly define and address them so that it can be quite clear how they derive from all we have already spoken about. The questions that follow will hopefully help to further inspire you to let go of any reserves you may have about affirming your happiness. The description of various kinds of unhappiness is by no means meant to be exhaustive, but rather brief suggestions of the truth that you are coming to know at this point: that all unhappiness is a belief, operative as a feeling, sometimes more or less intense depending upon the value we give to any specific instance. Fundamentally, it is a variant of the same basic belief, i.e., that you cannot escape feeling unhappy. Each instance of unhappiness may seem to be a different entity when, as we have seen, it is not. And keep in mind the ABC's as you go through this section. Unhappiness is strictly in the domain of "B" the realm where the issue of control of the world is raised. And remember, there is absolutely nothing wrong with wanting to control the world. The issue is solely one of making that control the necessary condition for your happiness. That's all. Okay off we go!

GUILT

Guilt is first, feeling bad about not feeling bad, when you believe it was appropriate to have felt bad, but you did not feel that way. For example, Mrs. Thistlewood tells you about Freddy's savage end and you really don't "feel bad" for her. She's a "kook" is what you think at the time. Later, however, you think that it was "wrong" of you not to have felt bad because kook or not, she was in pain over Freddy's demise and now you feel bad because you did not originally feel bad. Or, your Uncle Harry was feeling lousy last night at the party for your Aunt Sally, but you were too engrossed in hitting on that buxom blonde so you did not attend to him the way that you *should* have. Now, you feel bad for not having been more empathetic and appropriately pained by Harry's problems. You feel bad over not having felt bad.

Second, guilt is a prod and reminder that you should have been a way you were supposed to be and weren't. Certain behaviors and attitudes are supposed to trigger this feeling as a warning and a motivator either to avoid the behavior or just the opposite, to do a particular thing or be a way, attitudinally, that you are supposed to be. For example, you just made a golf date with the big corporate VIP that you rarely ever get a chance to socialize with and then later remember that you had promised to take the kids to the circus that afternoon. You feel bad about having to disappoint them because the career opportunity is what you are choosing over the time with the kids. You feel bad and troubled about the choice even as you pursue the golf date as planned.

Or, you are really enjoying talking to your son's Little League baseball coach. Since your husband is never available to be at the games, you spend a fair amount of time talking with Tom, the coach. You are charmed by his willingness to listen and feel yourself warming to his presence and his obvious commitment of time to children. This sense of pleasure immediately triggers a feeling of discomfort at having allowed that to happen with another man. It *shouldn't* have been and you feel bad about that.

Not to feel guilty would lead, it is believed, to unhappiness. Anyhow, to feel happy when you are supposed to feel unhappy is "evil." And "evil" is a way of being that it is assumed will make you unhappy. Therefore, guilt is seen as a "necessary evil" to prevent being "evil" and therefore unhappy!

QUESTIONS

- Do you believe that you have to feel bad or guilty over not having felt bad in order for you to be happy? Walk through a day with yourself and make note of every encounter where you became aware of not having been a way either you or others thought you were supposed to be, i.e., with your spouse, kids, at work, at play etc. As you can, open yourself up to questioning that belief through the Option Method.

- Use your understanding of the third Option Question so it applies here: do you think it would mean anything about you were you not to be unhappy, i.e., feel guilty about anything you may have done or failed to do? Take into consideration your understanding of the sections on *Time* and *Doing the Best you Can*, along with the other resources I mentioned as being helpful, i.e., *Joywords* and whatever other materials I might have available, i.e., *The Unbearable Wrongness of Being*, or *The Godspeak*, audio tapes, etc.

EXPER/CISES

- Take some time to examine experiences you have had with guilt. Have they led to more happiness in your life? Or, have you actually created more unhappiness for your self, as in becoming angry and resentful for somehow feeling you have to be guilty, i.e., unhappy, in order to be "okay" again with yourself or others.
- Look at your own motivations carefully. Don't you want what you want? What does feeling bad about your past actions do for you now? Don't you feel a greater clarity over the actions that you no longer have any intention of performing when this comes from your joy rather than from your pain? Write down your experiences with this exploration in as much detail as you like. Remember, this is your *personal* Journal and you are free to be totally open with yourself.

ANGER/RAGE/LIKING AND NOT LIKING

In anger the key component is the belief that a) either you or others or events were not being the way they were supposed to be and b) that should not have been the case, i.e., it should have been otherwise and you (they) should have known better. It is the feeling that something happened to us or to others and it was not supposed to happen. Somehow we were supposed to be able to control or know whatever it was we failed to control or know and now we have consequences that "shouldn't have been." By becoming unhappy in the form of anger, we supposedly provide ourselves or others with an admonishment and disapproval for not having been able to do or avoid whatever it was we were supposed to do or avoid. For example, Aunt Rose puts me in charge of watching the pasta. This is a great responsibility because God help me if the pasta is not "al dente" and is overcooked. But on one occasion when I was eleven, I was distracted from my solemn duties by my pretty cousin Angelina. The pasta was mush. Aunt Rose got extreme agita and pulled my ear, telling me I had a *lupo in capello* or roughly, I was an absentminded jerk. She was pissed. I *should* have been watchful. It shouldn't have happened that the pasta was overdone. Anger. It is so common an experience: you should have gotten up earlier and not been late for the meeting; you should have remembered it was your sister's birthday; you should have known that you would hit a massive traffic jam at that hour on the bridge, etc., etc.

Rage is the escalation of the feelings of anger often in response to a deepened sense that the universe, in the form of ourselves, other people or natural forces is beyond our control. The ostensible aim of anger is to focus the angry feelings so as to achieve some level of motivation to change ourselves or others. Of course, from my perspective this is an ineffective strategy. But in rage, even that pretense is lost and we fire blindly into the dark of the realization of our lack of control and flail about seething in our sense of being helpless to make the world be the way we say it has to be in order for us to give ourselves permission to be happy. Behaviors based on rage are often of the most destructive kind to self and others.

And, yes, it is the same old thing again. We fear **not** being unhappy in the form of anger, because without the anger we would not motivate ourselves to be the way we are supposed to be in order to be happy. Sounds familiar doesn't it? Yup. 'Tis the old refrain of "B" logic of the ABC's. I don't control the world, but, paradoxically, I must control at least some of the world in order to experience some happiness. Anger is just another strategy to pressure me into somehow being more skillful at controlling the world.

Now, often when we become angry, we later decide that the anger was either not legitimate or was excessive in some way. Then, of course, we feel guilty for having been a way we were not supposed to be. This can set up a cycle of anger/guilt/anger/guilt......because we can become angry at "having to" become unhappy in the form of guilt and we feel guilty, at having been wrongfully angry. Remember the unhappiness loop diagram. It works with all unhappiness in the sense that we tend to loop back through phases of our unhappiness until we end up back with the original feeling.

For example, you were just angry because your son did not clean his room. You yelled and screamed at him. This is the "umpteenth" time you have told him. *What is wrong with this kid that he doesn't show the slightest willingness to cooperate around here?* You call him names or suggest that he is less than a genius and so on. A little time passes. You calm down and begin to feel what? Yes that's right, you begin to feel bad, i.e., guilty, for having become angry with him. *What is wrong with you that you can't conduct yourself in a manner more conducive to creating an atmosphere of cooperation around here?* You feel bad for being a way you should not have been. You should have known better. It should not have happened. (Wow, I haven't seen such a line of "shoulds" in a long time.) But you go upstairs to make nice. He is not in his room and his room is still a mess. You begin to feel your ire rising again. *Damn it, I wouldn't get so angry if he would only cooperate. And who's responsible for my feeling guilty now anyway? I wouldn't have to go through this cycle if he would only be the way he is supposed to be to begin with.* Bingo! You are back to square one of the cycle. Your anger.

This cycle can amplify unhappy feelings towards ourselves, to the degree we see ourselves moving through an endless series of what look like self defeating behaviors that are not modified by either our anger or guilt.

Or, we can feel the same way towards other people or the world for the same reasons. But we know the world does not cooperate with our values on any predictable basis and we do not end up with all of what we want. Rage can be a result of, again, the feeling of being helpless to do anything about the way the world operates and believing that we have to be or are going to be made to be unhappy about it.

LIKING/NOT LIKING: This is an opportunity to apply Option to break the cycle. It does not mean that we have to accept the way the world is at any time. No, we are perfectly free to like or not like what has taken place or is taking place. We can do so with great passion and gusto. However those feelings have no unhappiness inherent in them. They simply arise comfortably, though not necessarily dispassionately, from our knowing and wanting what we like and not wanting and not liking what we don't like. We are free to do this and be happy. We are free to change our minds about our preferences. No reason is required. No explanation is required. The unhappy emotional charge that pushes not liking to anger is strictly a product of "B" logic.

For example, most of us do not like the notion of being caught in a traffic jam, or having to wait in a long line at the bank, or finding that the dog just deposited a gift on the living room carpet, or that your husband forgot to pick up the tickets for the theater on Saturday night, or your daughter has gotten herself pregnant, or your best friend has been stabbing you in the back with vicious gossip at work that might cost you a promotion, or that the way politics is run in this country is in your opinion abominable, or that people strap bombs to themselves and blow up other people as well, etc., etc.. These are all examples of how the world happens to be at any given moment in history. You are a part of history, of this very moment when all these things that you don't like are going on. Your control over them is marginal in most instances. According to the logic of "B" this inability to get things to conform to your notions of what is appropriate is the reason for your unhappiness, in the form of anger.

Again, the belief is that the unhappiness is necessary to capture some of that control. Without it you lose your grip and slip further down into helplessness.

But consider this: **In addition to whatever you may lose or fail to achieve or control in this existence, do you also want to surrender your happiness and joy? Think about it.**

So, if your likes or preferences, which is just another word for what you might want at any time, are not bound up with beliefs about "needs to control in order to be happy," then you are free to want without adding the "sting" of unhappiness, in the form of anger here, if you don't get what you want. Liking, preferring, or wanting comes from the **joy** of liking, preferring or wanting, not the **dread** of not getting. It may be mild or passionate depending upon what and how you may want what you want. You want a glass of water or you want your wife not to die of cancer. Your affection for what you want/like and your lack of affection for what you don't like can be absolutely clear to you and you can display your passion about that without any felt sense of distress or dis-ease over those wants/likes. The fear is that without the anger/distress to galvanize you into action, you will lack the necessary motivation to act on behalf of your liking and not liking, so that you will have only a tepid, indifferent existence and have very little success at getting much of what you want in the world.

Well, ask yourself, do I find my track record with anger and distress to be so formidable that I experience it as the way to be to get more joy in my life? I don't think that you would be reading this far in this book were that the case.

QUESTIONS.

- Would a failure to be angry about doing things that you don't like somehow be an admission that you really do like them?

- Would a failure to be angry about the people, things in the world (hunger, wars, human suffering of all sorts) that you do not love or like in any way mean that you would be endorsing those things?
- Is there any sense at all that without your anger you would be indifferent, uncaring? That without it, you would lack the requisite display of pain that would allow you to feel good about yourself?

EXPER/CISE

- Now I know it is fashionable to speak about "appropriate" anger, and other forms of "appropriate miseries" as well, but let me propose a little test. First, all unhappiness is what I call "context dependent." By that I mean that if you took what many people describe as "appropriate" unhappiness by whatever name, anger, grief, sadness, outrage etc., and deprived it of a specific context, then would you want to feel it? The context, as in the examples above, is everything in the world of "B" logic: sicknesses, losses, deaths, frustrations, failures, betrayals, etc., etc.
- What I want you to do is the following. Take one of those feelings that absolutely does **not** apply to anything in your life at the moment. Let's say anger. Now just "for the heck of it" go ahead and feel it! Yes that's right, I know there is no context or reason in this moment, but go ahead and try to put anger in your body anyway. How does it feel?
- My guess is that to the degree you are actually successful in doing so, it doesn't feel like anything you want to feel. Now some of you out there are attempting to conjure up anger by thinking of something in your past that made you angry. No, no, no! That is not what I want you to do. You are to put the feeling in your body **without** reference to any context! Got it now? Does it feel like anything you want to feel? No? Okay.

- Now, take any good feeling that you can think of, joy, elation, mellowness, satisfaction, tenderness, gratitude, humor, playfulness, deep comfort etc., etc. and put that into your body right now. Well, how about it? Any problems? I will bet to the degree that you have been successful, you have no objections to having those good feelings in your body *at any time*, context or no context. Okay, you are getting the point. Practice this exper/cise until this becomes crystal clear to you. **Unhappiness** you agree to feel only because there is a context that you believe requires its existence. So you feel it and "feel good" about having felt it in some instances because it was required and you were "right" to feel that way. **But happiness has no boundaries, no context it depends upon in order to be a legitimate, welcome way to feel.** You want it whenever you can get it and deny it to yourself only based on the beliefs that to feel it would be inappropriate under some circumstances. Correct? Okay.

The following exercises are designed not so much to address intense anger or rage, but to start with the smaller experiences of what we might describe as annoyances. These are minor instances of anger that many times never rise to the felt level of actual anger, much less rage, though in some cases they provide the ongoing irritation and provocation that can escalate and explode into the stronger emotions. So, what we have are everyday ways, in all the ordinary contexts that might evoke annoyance for you. Here, with less intensity to deal with, is an opportunity to change your experience. You may want to read the sections on *gratitude* and *wanting* to help establish how comfortable feelings can easily displace the discomforting ones when we become clear that we really want to do what it is we become annoyed at doing.

EXPER/CISES IN GRATITUDE FOR REMEMBERING:

- We are so often angry or annoyed that we forget things. But we only know we have forgotten when we remember. Isn't it strange that at the point of remembering, we become angry for discovering we have forgotten. When we leave the house and forget the keys to the car and only remember when we are sitting in the driver's seat realizing that we have no keys, why be angry? That is the moment when we find the wonder of how we are put together, that is we discover the great gift of **remembrance.** Whether it is the car keys, or your purse or wallet, your checkbook, credit card, doctor's, dentist's appointment etc., there is a whole new way of experiencing forgetting, and that is in the *joy of remembering*! Aren't you glad that you did remember? And don't you really want to drive the car, or make the purchase or keep the appointment? Remembering is in the service of helping you get what you want. So even though there may be consequences, i.e., walking back into the house to retrieve what you have lost, or some lost opportunity, still you can find gratitude in your recovering the knowledge of what you want. The anger or annoyance is an attempt to chastise or criticize yourself for being someone who would forget. Does the pain of annoyance and anger make you less likely to forget, or does it just fog up the clarity that you would otherwise have out of your joy?

- Take the many opportunities that each day gives to practice the joy of remembering. The first time you forget something and have to go back, even if you are then late etc., stop and sense the loyalty of you towards yourself in reestablishing the knowledge of what you have forgotten. Laughter and a smile *about yourself* is always a good way to establish a resonance of satisfaction with yourself. Remember, each moment is an opportunity to feel and experience your joy. ***There are no exceptions.*** The time you spend walking back to retrieve what you have forgotten, the time spent waiting in traffic, or on a bank line, those are actual moments never to be repeated again; they are opportunities for joy equal in being to standing on a beach watching the sunset or relaxing in your armchair listening to your favorite music.

NEEDING

The concept of need arises out of mistrust of ourselves. In Sections 8, 9 and 10 we addressed this notion and saw how the logic of "B" and a "need" to control the world were operative. Again, *motivation* is the key. As the authors of our own attitudinal destinies, we can come out of our happiness and exercise our freedom to want whatever it seems good for us to want. We can freely cooperate with our natural physical wants for food, sex, comfort and companionship. There is no "need" involved. For what is meant by "need" is the fear that if we do not motivate ourselves to cooperate with our physiology, if we do not move ourselves to find companionship, if we do not attempt to have some leverage or power in our social world, that then we will experience consequences. Now, it is true, if we don't have food we will die, if we don't have shelter we will be naked to the elements, if we don't have education, we will be ignorant of what knowledge the world may have, if we don't have financial means or social/political power, we will be poor and disenfranchised etc. But we fear those consequences because it is believed that if we suffer any of them, we will have to be unhappy about that! At the heart is fear of the consequences and fear of ourselves as somehow deficient in the motivation to avoid them or to acquire the means to fulfill our wants. It is simply a variant of feeling we need to be (and therefore, fearing that we will be) unhappy if we do not get what we want.

Thus *want* becomes "need" and immediately emphasizes thereby the lack of freedom or even the fear of freedom in our negotiating our wants in the world. We fear that out of our freedom we will, again, not find it in ourselves to be sufficiently motivated to control the world. The requirement to follow the iron "need to control in order to be happy" logic of "B" of the ABC's is paramount. 'Needs" are what **must** be, in order to avoid consequences that will bring unhappiness; ***wanting*** is knowing that we will affirm freely what we want and that we motivate ourselves fluidly and comfortably. However the world may or may not cooperate with what we value and want, our happiness and joy are never subject to being denied by those outcomes.

QUESTIONS

- Do you need to eat, or do you want to eat? If you want to eat, why would you call it a need? (Such a notion would be incomprehensible to Aunt Rose for whom eating was God's central gift of joy to his otherwise wretched human creatures!) If you do not wish the physical consequences of either not eating or eating too much, then why wouldn't you trust your wanting to be your guide? Are you afraid that, without the fear of becoming unhappy you will lack motivation because you have not fulfilled a need? Look at the section on addictions and self trust for further help.

- Do you want to love/live or do you need to love /live? The same logic as described in the previous question applies here. Clearly there is no need to either love or live, since people freely decide to love or not in specific contexts with others and they also decide to live or not within the boundaries of our biological lifespan (i.e., some commit suicide, most don't).

EXPER/CISES

- Make a list of items that you may now consider "needs." For example I "need" to love my children, make more money, eat less, stop taking drugs, be more affectionate with my spouse, start work earlier, call my folks regularly, exercise consistently, take time to smell the flowers, listen to good music, give myself some space each day to relax, etc., etc.. Take one item at a time and place it into the Option

Method understanding of "need." See what arises for you as you consider allowing the need to be what you want, without penalty or emotional coercion. Use the Option Method to deal with whatever arises out of this procedure. Enjoy the freedom that you gain each time you let go of a need and feel the freedom of trusting your own motivation to want. Write down your experience with each instance and see how your personal observations aid you more and more each time you come upon some "need" in your life.

HATE

Hate comes from a more deeply felt fear that someone or something can make you feel unhappy against your will. Such a person or thing then becomes the object of your loathing because they are seen to have that capability to destroy your happiness. "Enemy" is the word given to a person perceived to have such a potential. What an enemy wants is, at root, to destroy your happiness. That is why hatred often draws forth intense, sometimes physically violent or even deadly responses. What one perceives to be defending is their own happiness and sometimes it is believed only the destruction of the hated one will accomplish this. What is going on is of course simply fear. The way this enemy can destroy your happiness only you define, because you define what unhappiness is for you. This again is part of the logic of "B" of the ABC's. When you live from the truth of "C," then there can be no enemies, because no one and nothing can deprive you of your happiness. Naturally, of course, there can be people who intend you harm on many levels and you are perfectly free to do whatever you can to protect yourself from them.

Hatred is often the outcome of fearful loving. We often want to love someone, but the other person will not cooperate with our love by being the way they are supposed to be, from our perspective, so that we can love them. That failure to cooperate with our desire to love them we see as destructive to our happiness. By not responding, they are making us unhappy and we do not feel any control over that. Hatred, according to the definition just given is what we produce against such a person who now moves from an object of our love, to an object of fear, fear that we will have to suffer the unhappy consequences of their non-cooperation with our desires to love them.

Let us contrast that with *liking and not liking*, which are reflections of what we presently value and prefer and what we do not. We could know this without any kind of discomfort at all to motivate or deter us in any way. This is exactly what was written about earlier in the section on *Anger* which so often accompanies hatred, like peanut butter and jelly. As we have been saying, and will continue to state, they are branches from the same tree of unhappiness and have identical roots in the "B" logic of the ABC's.

QUESTIONS

- Do you fear that if you did not hate the people/groups/ideas that you hate, that you would somehow be approving of or liking the way that they are? That you would be validating and supporting something for which you have no love?

EXPER/CISES

- Make up an "enemies" list and examine your beliefs about whatever or whoever appears on the list. Each time you make a breakthrough to not liking rather than hating, cross the item off the list and celebrate your freedom from hate.

JEALOUSY/ENVY
FAIRNESS/UNFAIRNESS

It follows from the concept of hatred that our unhappiness about the world's non-cooperation with our wants and desires would breed a subset of hating calling jealousy and envy. We sometimes fear other people's happiness because we fear that they will be happy while we experience ourselves as unable to be that way. We don't want that. We would prefer that they fear their happiness so that they can join us in the "solidarity of the miserable." We may interpret their getting what they want to mean something about us. We have some deficit, some deficiency of motivation, we are lacking in what is needed to acquire the necessary persons, goods and services that will allow us to be happy. So not only are we unhappy and fearful of ourselves, but, as with hatred, we extend our ill will to those who have better fortune than we do. It may become intolerable for us to see others receive all the things we want and somehow cannot manage to have.

It can become clear how jealousy and envy can distort into pathways for the expression of hatred and even rage. Maybe you see the other as unworthy of getting what they wanted. Surely they have not been the way they were supposed to be sufficiently so that they deserved this. The sense of being a victim can enter in here as well. If you have been "good" in the sense of fulfilling the cultural norms, then you may feel deserving, more deserving than those who patently have not been as observant as you of those rules. Yet, these others may advance in the world and get more of what they want while you languish in the limbo of non-achievement despite your compliance with norms and rules. The words "fairness" and "unfairness" are brought in to heighten your sense of victimization. Unfairness means that you were "deserving" but you still did not get the recognition or receive what you wanted. Others did who were less so. The feeling of being cheated and victimized can grow intensely.

But what could "deserve" possibly mean? What actually happens is that you play by your own rules or the rules of society or some sub grouping of society and then you either get or don't get what you want. It could be that you promised yourself to take a vacation if you got a raise, and you didn't take it. You were promised tenure if you undertook a certain project for the Dean, but you didn't get it (something like that actually happened to me). You wrote what you thought was a brilliant essay for a class and still didn't get an "A." You made an agreement with your son about cleaning his room and he didn't follow through. Can't you just smell the logic of "B" of the ABC's here? Why? Because part of successfully controlling the world is making sure that you get what you "deserve." Right?

Now, sometimes of course people do cheat and victimize you, i.e., pick you out to be treated in a way that you do not want (look at Section 10 again), but sometimes we only imagine that this is the case and create "as if" conceptions of other people operating against our interests. (Reread the early part of section 10, *Fear of Being Bad For Yourself*) For example, we may believe that our best friend is spreading gossip about us, but in fact he/she is not. We may believe that the foreign words just spoken by a taxi cab driver are an insult when they actually are a greeting. We may believe that the cashier just shortchanged us but we actually dropped some of the money, so she did not. In either event, whether we are actually the objects of mistreatment or only think we are, we will be unhappy if we believe it somehow is supposed to be different in order for us to be okay with ourselves.

But we could know by now that once you remove the notion of getting what you want as the requirement for happiness, the entire picture can change instantly. We do not have to like the way the world and people in it are. Nature is arbitrary, or at a minimum inexorable in its alterations and motions, i.e., earthquakes, floods, droughts etc., and people are arbitrary as well in designating what and who is defined as "good" and "deserving" and who is not. What could "fairness" mean in the face of that truth? The setting up of rules and the carrying out of those rules in dealing with one another are of course a central way to promote good will and to encourage trust among humans. But as desirable as this may be, there is no guarantee that such rules will be observed uniformly by all. It is just another kind of "not getting what you want" when you find that those rules are not observed in the manner you desire. You are free to seek what redress you may, but the good news is, as always, that your happiness lies beyond a thing called "fairness" or "deserving." Others will decide the application of such words as they may, but your happiness is not what you deserve, not what is fair to you, but the very fabric of who you are and thus out of reach of the designs, ill will or machinations of anybody.

QUESTIONS

- On top of not getting what you want in some particular instance, do you also want to feel unhappy about it?
- Are you fearful that unless you are unhappy in the form of envy or a sense of being unfairly treated, i.e., victimized or cheated, you will not be sufficiently motivated to redress the situation and get what you want if you can?

EXER/CISES

- Locate yourself in your world with some exactitude. That is, define how you see yourself, i.e., as father, mother, child, employee, craftsman, professional person, concerned citizen, etc. In all these instances, the world has sets of rules, imperatives, behaviors that it holds up as required or desired ways to be. Despite attempting to live up to those expectations, you may not feel sufficiently acknowledged or rewarded. See the degree to which any of those roles involve a sense of envy, victimization, feelings of unfairness etc. Deal with each instance using the Method. See how by doing so you gradually begin to transcend any role you have created for yourself and any fear that by not getting what you want in any of those roles you somehow are having your access to your happiness limited. Record your experiences in detail.

ADDICTION/PANIC ANXIETY/OBSESSIONS/COMPULSIONS

There are several dimensions to such experiences. Many times, the person has accepted the notion that it is not all right to be cautious about how they run their lives. They have bought into some version of having to be some way others want them to be so that they will be acceptable. They believe that, if they follow their own sense of caution and do not behave in ways demanded of them, they will lose the love and support of people around them. We can all remember experiences when we were young where we were challenged to do things or be a way that we felt uneasy about. Instead of listening to our own voice, many times, out of fear of being called a "chicken" or "wimp," we engaged in the activity, i.e., we climbed the tree or water tower, swam out in water over our head, pretended to be comfortable in social situations where we were not welcome.

We do this following the logic of "B" of the ABC's because we believe we have to control or master our environments and that we do not have a right to stand back from situations and wait until we feel we have satisfied our inner sense of caution with more trustworthy information. It is one thing to encourage inquisitiveness and exploration, and it is another to try and force us into societal/familial programs or behaviors that may be out of sync with our own personal sense of what is best for us. For most of us who engage in this ignoring of our own sense of caution, through the premature adoption of ways of being simply to satisfy the logic of "B," the result may be anxiety experiences of varying degrees. For some who may be physiologically disposed, the result can be an intense bodily event called a panic attack or compulsion/obsession. Others may utilize mind altering substances to ameliorate the anxieties that come from trying to control the world and find themselves locked in a physiological cycle for which there does not seem to be an exit.

Inside the experiential world of that cycle, compulsions/obsessions, and panic/addiction create a feeling in your body that you believe you must respond to in a certain way in order to avoid unhappiness. Utilizing some substance that seems to quiet the physical feeling or limiting your movements in the world so as to avoid what seems the spontaneous outbreak of panic, or observing some rituals of fulfillment or avoidance are the answer on a very short term basis, until the effect wears off and the same physical feeling returns. However, like everything else, we merely believe this physical feeling has the power to make us unhappy. We fear what it could mean and we believe we are trapped by the only apparent solution, i.e., the utilization of whatever substance or avoidance strategy that we have learned will quell that feeling and bring short term euphoria, or merely relief of the feeling.

The answer is the same, that is to get out of the logic of "B" and move to the logic of "C" of the ABC's. If we are willing to sustain our sense that whatever the physical feeling, we are free to respond or not respond and that our happiness is not dependent upon responding in any particular way, then our physiology will cooperate by gradually extinguishing the physical signal that seems to require our response. This is how all people let go of addictions, compulsions, obsessions, and panic experiences. There are pharmaceutical, nutritional, herbal aids that can ameliorate the physiological aspects of this experience and there is no reason not to make yourself as comfortable as possible while you recover from such experiences. However, the key element is knowing that nothing that your body can produce in response to its external or internal environment can deny you access to your happiness.

QUESTIONS

- What do you most want for yourself, the brief reprieve or high that you may attain by the substances or rituals you employ, or an ongoing sense of joy?
- If you were to do what your mind or body seems to be telling you to avoid doing, or, conversely, not do what your mind or body seems to be telling you to do, what would be the outcome? Whatever your answer, ask yourself if you believe you have to be unhappy about that?

EXER/CISES

- Your body as part of you is doing the very best it knows to do given the information that it has about how to proceed. Even when you do not like the results of your body's efforts, can you begin to acknowledge the truth of the first statement? Is it not true that just as you want to have peace of mind you also want peace of body? Would you be willing to do whatever it takes to achieve both? Experiment with having compassion for the pain of your body's urges and cravings while at the same time not responding to them or interpreting them as requiring you to do something about them.
- Would it be okay with you to be happy with yourself right now in this moment, even though you may not have resolved any or all of the issues around your anxiety or panic? This is fundamental, because happiness is always now and it is always for you as you are now, not as you might be in some hypothetical state of personal achievement. Go ahead and be with your happiness now no matter what else is going on in your life or where you are in your efforts to let go of various habits and beliefs. Take the time to record individual instances of success at doing this.

GOOD/BAD

Good or Bad are basically pragmatic, utilitarian appraisals about whether something does or does not serve to help us in our dealings with the world. A wrench may be good for loosening bolts but bad when used as a paintbrush. Tomato sauce may be good with pasta but bad with risotto. A few days of rain may be good for the crops, but three weeks of rain will be bad for them. Words like "need" **do** have a place in the workaday vocabulary we use. If we want to create water, then we **need** to combine hydrogen and oxygen in certain proportions. If we want to move that boulder, then we **need** to or **must** apply a certain amount of force. If we put yeast in our dough, our bread **should** rise. When we are talking about the world and our desire to control or manipulate it, the "B" of the ABC's, then we have to play by the laws of physics that *require* certain kinds of activities, ingredients etc., in order to bring about desired effects. That is technology and we gradually become more capable of utilizing the complexities of the world for fun and profit. That's fine.

However, that is not how good and bad are normally perceived when it comes to the issues of happiness or values. They are used to represent states of being and behavior that we are either supposed to exemplify or avoid. The implication is that if we are not "good" then we will not have the right to be happy. And, if we are "bad," then we somehow will end up unhappy by virtue of being in that state. All this blends in together with the notions of unhappiness that we have already seen when we turn from the pragmatic dimensions of the "B" hypothesis and make control of the world a requirement for our joy. Thus, we fear being "bad" because it is seen as a way of being capable of depriving us of our happiness. We also fear not having the appropriate motivation to be "good" and thereby not qualifying for permission to be happy. Good and bad turn into judgments that we use against ourselves or others to keep ourselves in line with our values or to identify what in ourselves or others contradicts our values and therefore threatens our happiness. A bad person can easily fall into the category of "hated" and have all the implications that that description carries (reread the section on *Hate* above).

The problem also is that there is absolutely no way to get rid of "good" and "bad" used this way once you have introduced them as outcomes of the moral logic of the "B" hypothesis where your worth, value, or "goodness" is linked to your ability to achieve certain outcomes or measures of control in the world. The reason is that "bad" or "evil" become concepts that people appeal to in order to explain why they are unhappy. Following the descriptions found in the sections on *Hatred* and *Anger*, we often believe that others have the power to make us feel unhappy against our will. Once we adopt this value perspective as an explanatory system, then, we trap ourselves inside its false logic and resort to blaming and demonizing others as the cause of our distress.

Those values will be one thing for "Nazis" another for "Communists," still another for "Capitalists," and another for fundamentalist Christians, Muslims, Buddhists etc. You will end up as some version of being "evil" for those groups depending upon your unwillingness (or your genetic incapability, if it is a racial ideology) to conform to their version of "good." "Evil" is what being "bad" (in one of those visions of life) can lead to. And remember, "evil" can easily make you worthy of being destroyed as a member of an "impure race" or "class enemy" or "enemy of Christ," or "infidel," etc.

Only by getting out of the "trance logic" of "B" to embrace the truth of "C," i.e. that you do control the attitude you take toward whatever the world presents to you, can you step out of the cycle of "good" and "bad." By "trance" I mean the way beliefs manifest as unexamined, habitual responses and behaviors. They have an "automatic" character, which often makes it appear as if they somehow have a life of their own outside the authority of the person experiencing them. This in turn can add to the burden of believing that so much about us is beyond our control. Thus, again, we are seen as creatures of the world subject to its whim about our emotional existence.

QUESTIONS

- Do you have any fear that, without the judgments of "good" or "bad" as part of how you see the world, you would somehow fall prey to being ways that would deprive you of your happiness? For example if you did not judge people who commit crimes as "bad" even though you support the legal consequences for their actions, that somehow you would being "bad" yourself and have no right to your happiness?

- Do you believe that unless you feel bad (unhappy) about being "bad" (being ways others may disapprove of and label "bad") or not "good" enough (living up to standards and values that others define as necessary ways to be) that you will be unworthy or not have a right to be happy? In other words if you fail someone else's expectations of how you are supposed to be—caring, affectionate, responsible, hardworking, attentive, involved, communicative, committed, apologetic, sorry, sad, socially active, politically informed, sufficiently outraged or indignant etc., etc.,—that you have no claim on your happiness until you do conform to those expectations?

EXPER/CISES

- Take a newspaper and read through it. See what your reactions are to local and world events and to what degree "good" or "bad" plays a role in what you read. If any beliefs about how the way others are depicted brings up any sense or fear that their being that way could deprive you of your happiness, then use the Option Method to examine that myth.

- Make note of how you might be using good or bad as judgments. Review the sections on doing the best we can and on Judgments as well as other resource materials. See how good it feels to be free of these notions used to limit access to our joy.

LONELINESS/ RELATIONSHIPS

Our understanding of relationships and involvement with others is largely based upon our beliefs about unhappiness. Everything about unhappiness is tied in with the central visions outlined earlier according to which you **must** control the world, in this case your access to people and your ability to maintain those relationships in the logic of the "B" hypothesis of the ABC's. Relationships are simply part of that control trance logic. We can say that we want to be engaged with people, some more intimately than others. This comes from our freedom and joy in life and our desire to share our experience with others in ways that range from mild acquaintanceships to intense love. So far so good. But we already know that wanting is not enough for those of us who believe in unhappiness. It is an insufficient motivator. The comfort of wanting is transformed into the dis-ease and anxiety of "needing" others, needing their love and companionship. Now our happiness is at stake in getting what we want! Whereas when we are living out of our joy, being by ourselves never is tinged with dread, even though we might prefer the company of others.

Believing that we "need" others in order to be happy, fulfilled, complete etc., we dread being alone, a state we describe as "lonely," or simply, unhappy about being alone. We wonder if we will have the necessary motivation to engage with others so that we will have what we "need." The fear is that we will never be loved, or even deeper, as we have seen in the Section on *Motivation*, that we somehow might be deficient in the desire **to be** loved. What can contribute to this also is our fear that we are unlovable, that if people really knew us they would not want us (we will talk more about this when we deal with Love). Doubting our own self worth then, we lose heart, i.e., the motivation to even dare to want to be loved.

THE SELF DEFEATING RELATIONSHIP LOOP
This is an example of how our unhappiness about being alone and our desire to be with another can be twisted by our unhappiness into a self defeating loop. It does not cover all the variations that can occur in such cases, but it gives the general overall flavor of how such relationship loops operate.

1.Our initial feeling of loneliness or being unhappy about being alone, can prompt

8.Now we flee back to our original position of loneliness with even more cynical, negative feelings about the possibility of love, while at the same time still feeling trapped by "needing" a relationship

2. a desire to be with another which is turned into a "need" since we don't trust mere wanting to be a sufficient motivator to get us what we want.

3. The fear that the need won't be fulfilled leads one initially to downplay one's own preferences and cater to the wants of the other in hopes that this will prompt them to be more the way we say they have to be so that we can give ourselves permission to love them [i.e., be happy with them].

7.The intensities grow to the point where we "must" stop the pain of the price we feel we are paying for a relationship. Extreme solutions can be violent, but most often we feel only distaste for the other and for ourselves so we use any pretext of the others "bad behavior" to finally leave. We feel "forced" to do so.

4.When whatever strategies we use are unsuccessful, we become angry because the other person is not responding by being the way we wish. Yet at the same time we may be ever more fearful that they may leave us because we are now becoming unpleasant in our demands and accusations and they may somehow see how unworthy we are to be loved.

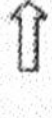

6.We begin to hate the other person for "making" us feel anger toward them and for helping to reveal to ourselves the depths of our feelings of unworthiness or inability to love or be loved.

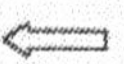

5. We begin to dread and hate ourselves for somehow being defective or lacking in whatever we believe we should possess that would somehow "make" the other person love us. We may feel guilty for being so angry with them over their failure to respond.

Why attempt to get love when rejection has inevitably to mean emotional pain and suffering? Again this all works in an unhappiness loop or cycle that can leave us numb, paralyzed by fear in the face of our desire for love and what we believe are the necessary pains if we don't get what we want. See here of course *The Self Defeating Relationship Loop*, which will specify a form of the unhappiness loop that hopefully will illustrate the way the issue of loneliness/relationships can be distorted by our unhappy beliefs. It will be relevant when we talk in the next section about relationships from the perspective of negotiating the "deal" that exists always in some form between people and in a special way between people seeking a loving accommodation with another. The logic of "B" is clearly operating in this loop. Believing we are so full of shortcomings, it is easy to see how the belief that we will betray our need for loving by such deeply rooted deficits, can grow to panic proportions. Everything around being with others, then, can become burdened with this dread and anxiety. We fear being caught between the dread of being alone and the trapped, frustrated feelings coming from thrusting ourselves into relationships that are primarily insurance policies against loneliness rather than open, comfortable explorations of how we can build joy together with others.

When we are so filled with self-doubt about our own worth, when we fear ourselves and believe that we can be against ourselves and our happiness, then it is easy to see how we can build up a picture of ourselves as unattractive, not merely physically (which is totally arbitrary anyway) but more importantly, in terms of our traits of character. We fear that others may come to discover our hidden deficits and be repulsed by our shortcomings. Often, then, we are not honest in building relations with others, lest they reject us and we find ourselves alone. Honesty can be a casualty of our attempt to keep others from knowing us. Since we have decided we "need" others, we can be willing to live in situations where we are deeply dissatisfied yet even more afraid of losing the companion should we fully reveal ourselves out of our freedom and joy. Our love becomes highly conditioned by our fears and we often live in severely limited encounters with others just to preserve the relational link.

So many other forms of unhappiness can enter the picture to intensify our misery: *guilt* over not being honest, **anger** towards ourselves and the other person who is seen as potentially rejecting the person we fear we really are; *hatred* of ourselves and the other person for similar reasons; *blame* of ourselves and judgment of the others; living without love for some sense of **debt** or **obligation** to another; and a sense of *failure* or even loss of the opportunity to somehow be happy.

QUESTIONS

- Are you afraid that you would endanger your chances to attract people if you were not sufficiently uncomfortable about enjoying being alone, or even periods of solitude?
- While of course you do not "owe" anyone information about yourself, do you fear sharing in ways you feel appropriate—the full breadth of how you actually experience yourself to be, particularly your openness and sense of joy without limit?
- Do you fear to lose the community of fellow humans if you do not yield to their demands to be unhappy in certain circumstances, i.e., as when they are unhappy, your unhappiness becomes a pledge and sign of your humanity and empathy? Hint: you cannot feel bad about or for somebody else *unless* you would feel bad about it happening to you. Ask yourself: would *I* be unhappy about that if it happened to me? Remember, to live your joy now is not to be without loving concern for others.

EXPER/CISES

- If you do not find your relations with others satisfactory and are unhappy about them, review each one using the Option Method.

See the degree to which your fear of being alone is used as a motivator to maintain relationships.

- Take some time out for solitude and lovingly observe what kinds of concerns come up in that state. Focus on the joys of being with yourself and respond to any objections in the form of thoughts or unhappy feelings that might arise as you allow yourself to enjoy your own company.

- If you are in relationships that you find unsatisfactory, experiment with more honesty in revealing yourself and your feelings. Do so in ways that are nonjudgmental and, if you can manage it, fun-filled or playful. Even if they are not accepted by the other, see the degree to which you can feel freer and more joyful no matter what the outcome of your efforts.

NEGOTIATION/ THE "DEAL"

This section is devoted to a brief overview of how Option might work in helping to disentangle some of the problems that arise between people who are seeking a way of living lovingly together. First, let me make clear that from my perspective, all work with people is individual work. There is no "couples" work as such even though I do work with people as couples and in groups to help accomplish what they have already in some measure achieved in finding out the truth of their personal happiness in individual work with me. But, what is primary from the Option Method perspective is the personal happiness of the individual. Again, from the lessons of the "ABC's" we know that all we control is our own attitudinal destiny; all else is subject to the laws of physics or, in the case of dealing with another human being, with the ways in which that person goes about dealing with their attitudinal destiny.

Option can be invaluable in building a relationship however because to the degree that the people involved are focusing on their own personal happiness, to that degree they may find a much greater readiness to enter into the only useful form of discourse that can occur between humans, i.e., negotiations or dialogue. So, once you leave the realm of your own personal happiness, then your main tool for navigating the world around is negotiation. Now it takes just a moment to reflect and realize this is the truth. The crucial question is, then, how you enter those negotiations. If you enter with a whole boatload of demands, imperatives and ultimatums that are unbending and non-negotiable, then the likelihood of a resolution and evolution is nil unless you are willing to simply capitulate and accept the agenda of the other person.

It is important to note that I have absolutely nothing to say about how people go about arranging their lives. That is their business. My business, in so far as people request it of me, is to guide them to affirm their happiness using the Option Method. So, the only thing, as I see it, that is non-negotiable as you enter into a negotiation/dialogue with another, is your own personal happiness. If you are happy with the outcome of your negotiations with another, then that is fine with me. I am not here to define what shape your existence should take. Of course what actually happens is that when a person comes to me and makes progress in using the Method to achieve greater happiness, they often bring in issues involving some important other person or persons as part of what they explore about what they feel makes them unhappy. Sometimes those other people will come and make the same kind of exploration for themselves. Then it can happen that two people are coming from a much better place with regard to their own happiness and so many of the issues and problems that caused distress between them are settled by their own change of attitude. They see through the "voodoo" talk of "needs" and other ways people have of caging themselves in the prisons of their assumptions, all the while longing helplessly, as they experience it, for the love and affections of another. You can reread the earlier preceding comments on *Loneliness and the Self Defeating Relationship Loop* to refresh your understanding.

What remains are the pragmatic, everyday issues and events that people encounter. With good will and a better sense of their own happiness, it is so much simpler to enter a negotiation/dialogue without fear and dread. ***Everything in life after your personal happiness is negotiation.*** Despite how the world would like to portray reality, there are no hard and fast rules about anything, there is no way things should or shouldn't be. So being in negotiation with another, one can make what I call **"the deal"** which is a living, evolving agreement about how two people want to live together, what rules and values will guide them and most importantly, a commitment to continue to dialogue and keep alive their awareness of the deal they have made. Now, everybody does have a "deal" with other people in their life; it can be a very small one as with, say, your auto mechanic or very intense and complicated, as with your spouse. The "deal" is an extension of the "deal" imposed upon people by culture/ideologies/religions etc. Think of the marriage vows in the Christian tradition. They spell out a deal. As always, though, those static ideals represented in ritual "deals" set up to support a society's goals, fall far short in most cases of satisfying the many layered assumptions that two people bring together in terms of expectations, "needs," demands and wants of every kind. No static deal can hope to create an adequate vessel for containing and providing the necessary forum for alterations that all such deals ultimately require to remain relevant and to have a chance of being a satisfying ongoing solution for two people seeking mutual felicity. What we know from our understanding of how people operate out of their unhappiness is that for so many people the deal is not explicit. People fear to make their wants and desires clear to the other party. They expect the other person to somehow divine what they want and claim to "need." So the hidden agendas of unacknowledged deals cause chronic dissatisfaction and disaffection. Again, unquestionably, the "deal" will change over time. What it is now at age 25, will be different at age 40 and still different at age 65 etc. Our views of things change; our sense of priorities and values will alter. The obvious difference between the hidden deals built on the unhappy beliefs of people, and the open deal we are talking about is that the latter, when people are coming from greater happiness, is visible and accessible for full discussion. If we maintain a loyalty to negotiation/dialogue and "the open deal," then it is likely that whatever comes up will have a high probability of being successfully resolved within the context of continuing to be with one another.

Let me emphasize again, that everything is potentially up for negotiation except one's personal happiness. However, as you no doubt understand by now, what most folks do is bring their happiness to the table as a bargaining chip. You see that in such phrases as "If you really loved me you would.....," or "You make me unhappy by......," and so many more that we have looked at in our examination of unhappiness thus far. When you put your happiness on the line in any negotiation, when you engage in the voodoo talk of pseudo-causality, "You make me angry, you make me miserable, you make me sad, you are responsible for my unhappiness" etc., the negotiations turn into a trial where it is necessary to convict the accused [your partner] of the high crimes and misdemeanors of causing you unhappiness. You hope, thereby, to sentence the partner to a period of repentance and amendment that will make him/her more the person that he/she has to be in order for you to give yourself permission to be happy. As we have seen, however, more often than not, the repentance and amendment only breed resentment for being the identified "schmuck" in the relationship and such strategies usually backfire. Trials, after all rarely are the breeding grounds for happy outcomes. Even when guided by a therapist so that both parties admit their "crimes" before the judge [the therapist] the outcome is doubtful because believing you cause unhappiness in others is a predisposing factor for becoming unhappy because you feel that happiness or unhappiness either in yourself or another is something that "happens to you" not something you control. Also, guilt at somehow being the cause, even if against your own will as it were, of the misery of another can compound the feelings of anguish and helplessness here.

So, the value of the Option Method can be enormous in aiding people who are open to affirming their happiness succeed in arranging a comfortable, and from their point of view, equitable "deal" where the tool of negotiation/dialogue will assure a state of openness and transparency between them that is the foundation stone of honesty and trust. Love has no problem growing and prospering in such a free and dynamic atmosphere.

Let me note finally that exiting or abrogating "the deal", however it may seem arbitrary to the other person, is your business. Your happiness does not depend upon the keeping or the breaking of any deal you make with another. However, it stands to reason that if what you want in this world is a loving accommodation with another, then the trust that sustains such an arrangement comes primarily from the spontaneous gift of your love for the other and the degree to which in accord with that love you are willing to create the tradition of negotiation and dialogue that opens your heart more fully to the other as an ever growing, more profound gesture of your willingness to share who you are with less and less reservation. Your birthright is to know your happiness and to affirm it; entering into a loving relationship with another is an opportunity for both parties to both know and be known through their love. The interplay of that intertwining of loving interests supports each person's playing in the world and achieving greater and more consistent levels of joy and all the intensities beyond.

QUESTIONS

- Are you aware of what your "deal" is with your partner or significant others?
- If not, are you willing to make it explicit?
- Are you aware of making your happiness hinge on the outcome of negotiations/dialogues you have with your partner?

EXPER/CISES

- Take some time to write down what you understand your "deal" to be with your partner. Obviously it would be best if both of you engage in this exercise and then compare notes.

- If possible, open up the "deal" to loving scrutiny so that you both know clearly what is contained therein. See the degree to which you both may have hidden agendas where your happiness is on the line if the other person doesn't abide by whatever the "deal" presently is. Use the Option Method to question assumptions that are problematic and see the degree to which you can clear up misunderstandings and bring yourself to a state of clarity about what you really want from the other person and what they want from you. By being able to affirm the primacy of your personal happiness, you can create the trust and honesty that may have been missing. Whatever the outcome, stay in touch with what you know now about the truth of your happiness.

JUDGMENTS/BLAME/RIGHTEOUSNESS

Judgments are beliefs about the ability of ourselves or others to deprive us or others of our happiness through the act of judgment. How often do we feel unhappy or anticipate feeling that way when we know others will disapprove of what we do. How about when we were kids and our mothers would say: "Just wait until your father gets home and hears about what you did today." I am not talking about getting a beating either (although that may have been part of your experience as a child as well), but the mere thought of having someone you care about look at you with that disapproving face. It connects with what we said about the concept of being "bad" (hopefully you will begin to notice that all these notions are intimately related because as we said at the outset of this section, all unhappiness is basically the same concept seen so many different ways). When you believe others have the power to deprive you of your happiness, then you can understand how judging comes in as just another aspect of that experience.

Remember, as part of the logic of "B," we do not control the world. So, as I have said many times thus far, we attempt to control as much of the world as we can in order to get permission to feel as much happiness as our beliefs will allow us to feel if we are successful at that task. However, when we fail to measure up to our own or others' expectations then we do (or are subject to) a thing called judging. In this manner we identify others or they identify us as having failed to measure up to some standards we or they believe in. In doing so, we have exhibited behaviors that render us unworthy to feel joy or happiness. By judging ourselves or others, we are fulfilling our roles to uphold the moral logic of those standards. Now we who failed to fulfill our duties are put on notice that we should ***not dare*** to take any unauthorized pleasure out of our behavior and indeed that we should exhibit some form of discomfort to demonstrate that we are sorry for our failures.

Judgments are different then from merely liking or not liking because they contain that core fear that unhappiness may result from what we ourselves or others may do. This relates, of course, to the notion that by not being a way we or others are supposed to be, our happiness is threatened. Thus judgments are like guilt, anger, hate, good, bad, that is, ways of motivating ourselves and others to be the ways that we are supposed to be so that we can avoid greater unhappiness or we can have permission to be happy now.

Blame is a judgment that we render *after* something has occurred and we have not gotten what we want, or we have gotten unwanted consequences from our own or others' actions. We identify something in ourselves or others as being the cause of our unhappiness. Again, feelings like guilt, anger, hatred etc. can accompany blame. Blame often is accompanied by the further judgment that we or others are "bad," that is, toxic to our own or others' happiness. If we are "bad," we can cause ourselves or others to feel a way we don't want to feel **against our will!**

Righteousness is the state of giving ourselves permission to feel good about having felt bad over how people have not been the way they were supposed to be and *we* were the ones who identified that or joined others  in doing so through judging. I recall the time when Aunt Rose discovered that the widow Manzoni was having an affair with the married shoemaker, Marco. Oh how she savored each detail and delivered the information with such triumph to the other ladies of her group over coffee and biscotti one afternoon(I was hiding behind the couch and understood enough dialect to catch the whole act of righteousness in full blossom). How bad and sad she felt for Marco's wife Tomasina, and how outraged she was that "snake" Manzoni (whom she professed she never liked even when her husband Antonio was alive. Just think of what she might have been doing then, God forbid!) had suceeded in working her charms. It's true Manzoni was a superior cook to Tomasina and Aunt Rose had warned her to come over and learn how to properly make *tumala* (a Sicilian baked stuffed pasta dish) since that was Marco's favorite dish. But did she listen to the warning. No. And now look what happened.

Okay, so, often a state like "moral outrage" is an experience of feeling bad, that then renders us worthy of feeling good, i.e., righteous. When a religious fundamentalist discovers someone not wearing the appropriate clothing, as in the experience of the Taliban morality police punishing both men and women for such infractions, or missing a required ritual; when a Nazi discovers a Jew hiding in a cellar; when a public figure is found to be dishonest; when we discover that our neighbor is having an affair etc.—then we can feel the pain of outrage which gives the promise of feeling the exhilaration of righteousness!

Again, in all of these categories, we can see the links with other states of unhappiness, with fear of being bad for ourselves, with a sense that we somehow should be able to have been other than the way we know to be in any given moment. We could know that there is no requirement for us to feel bad because we or others have **been** ways that do not cooperate with our values in *this* moment. This does not deny responsibility for our actions (See Section 10, *Fear of Being Bad For Ourselves,* among others).

Covenants and laws apply that may bring us or others consequences for our actions. We may or may not agree with how a particular society sets up its covenants and laws and we may not agree with the consequences that apply to various actions. However, that has nothing to do with our happiness. We can have gratitude that public order and the well being of individual members of society are at least to some degree being served by those strictures. If we are fortunate to live in a participatory democracy, then we are free to work to alter those laws and strictures that we might find against our values. But nowhere in this way of living is it necessary to surrender our good feelings by being unhappy over our own or others' behavior.

Indeed, our joy will be the most vital element in our ability to alter things about ourselves that we might not like and may have untoward social consequences. Remember in the section on *Doing the Best We Know to Do,* we explored this. Reread it. You may begin to understand that it is human unhappiness in all its dimensions that generates most of these untoward behaviors. Of course, since there are so many conflicting claims about how we are supposed to be, we would have to come to some agreement on some basic norms that would provide safety and liberty for humans. Surely, though, by getting past the limitations inherent in deriving our visions of human equanimity from the "B" logic of control and moving on to embrace more of the understanding of happiness through the "C" logic of joy we would have a clearer frame of mind in which to do that. The same would apply to our attitude towards those who cause *us* unwanted consequences. Though we may agree with the strictures applied as a result of their behaviors, we are free from any required pain of outrage or hatred to get on with our lives and build our joy from moment to moment.

QUESTIONS

- Would it feel strange for you to let go of judging/blaming yourself or others over things that you do not want or have no love for?
- Are you afraid in any way that, by not judging or blaming yourself or others, you would be approving of behaviors you do not want? Do you believe that these discomforting feelings are necessary to restrain yourself and others and that without them you would be inviting chaos or anarchy, that is, situations that could somehow deprive you of your happiness?

EXPER/CISES

- Take the daily newspaper and peruse the headlines. See whether what is written draws forth any feelings of judgment. Take note of this and take time to work with each item that seems to do this for you.
- Take part or all of a day and be aware of the degree that you might be judging yourself or others, your spouse, children, coworkers, people in the headlines, in your daily activities. Take some time when you can to note this and write out your responses using the Option Method to deal with the unhappiness that may be there for you.

OWING/OBLIGATION/DEBT

Do you believe that you owe yourself or anyone else anything? What could that mean? Many might immediately think of financial debts that we are said to owe to banks or individuals. It is true that such transfers of money are often accompanied by a huge amount of paperwork that stresses in assertive legal language the notion that by receiving this money you now stand under a strong obligation to repay it with interest or consequences will apply. Ah, the consequences. Well, in the case of money, the consequences might be the loss of income or property as a result of non-payment. However, when we speak of owing, obligation or debt in an emotional sense, what could the consequences of non-fulfillment of such arrangements possibly be? Yep. You guessed it. Loss of happiness, of course! Even when it comes to banks and other impersonal institutions, the ideals of public morality would brand you (judge you) to be "bad" for not repaying the money, though the emotional consequences are not always so clear.

However, when it comes to **emotional** debts and obligations, the judgments are much more forceful in their identifying you as "bad" for not being the way you are supposed to be. This is just another motivating strategy to try to make sure we get what we want, following the "B" logic of controlling the world, and the people in it as much as possible. Attempting to bind others by having them somehow internalize emotional promissory notes is a way of trying to make certain they remain or become a way that we say they must be in order for us to be happy. Again, we fear that by using our wants to guide our behavior, we will be insufficiently motivated to do things or be ways that we or others deem necessary for our happiness. Thus like *need,* owing, obligation and debt are created somehow to force ourselves and others to conform to our wants.

We know that by introducing these coercive concepts into the stream of our wanting, our lives are not improved. When we try to make our love companions feel that they owe us their love and emotional allegiance, does that improve or degrade the quality of our love for them and theirs for us? When we do not trust the freedom of our wanting to produce the results we want, we resort to the mechanisms of unhappiness to attempt to get what we want. We have seen time and again that unhappiness used as a motivator only produces more unhappiness. Children who feel indebted to their parents will color their love responses with overtones of guilt, anger, resentment and sometimes a begrudging fulfillment of such emotional obligations, one without the joy of freely giving their love.

Indeed, love that is not freely given, but bound by requirements that others become unhappy if our wishes are not fulfilled, is a very limiting love indeed and one whose strategies of unhappiness will often backfire. That is not to say that we cannot decide when and how we will love others and place limits on what we will accept as responses to our love. But that has nothing to do with *requiring* that others *become unhappy* if they do not fulfill the profile of what we want in love relationships.

I recall Aunt Rose's constant berating of her husband, my Uncle Joe (he was five feet four inches and weighed about 140 lbs., to her five feet nine inches and over three hundred pounds). She would always remind him that he had pursued her after the death of her first husband, and that he did so not only because of her considerable physical charms, which had grown even more considerable over the years, but also because of her unparalleled reputation as a cook. So that whether he was in bed or at the kitchen table, he was a man of enormous good fortune that not even the local Don Vincenzo Maggio could lay claim to with all his wealth and power. Then she would deliver the summation of her weekly proclamation of being wronged and disappointed with a speech that always went roughly like this (naturally including a few changes to suit current happenings in their lives):

"You promised me a good life, you promised me a trip back to Italy every two years, you promised me a charge account at Edmundo's butcher shop (Aunt Rose declared it the best one outside of Italy), you promised we would move closer to my daughters. What did you deliver? Niente! (Nothing!) You have no sense of debt and honor. I can't even lift my head up at mass in the morning, I'm so embarrassed that everyone knows I married a man who does not fulfill his obligations and has let me down so badly." Tears and moans would ensue. It would always end with his crying out '*Basta* (enough), folding his newspaper and going off to play bocci and drink wine with his fellow suffering male compatriots.

That can be the picture when we try to bind people to us out of fear. The vision offered in this book, and later explored in more detail in the section on *Love*, is that we offer our love in freedom, though perhaps with conditions on how we want others to be in response. If we do not get what we want, we can freely withdraw our love without blame or recrimination of any kind and remain non judgmentally inclined with good will towards the person who chooses not to be the way that we want them to be.

QUESTIONS

- Do you feel emotionally indebted to anyone? If so, examine why using the Method.
- Are you fearful of letting go of any sense of obligation or owing anyone, including yourself? Indeed, in the light of what you have just read, what could "owing" yourself possibly mean?

EXPER/CISES

- Take a piece of paper and write down all the emotional "debts" you feel you have pending in your life: to yourself, children, parents, friends, society etc. Next to each debt, work out a resolution using the Method. When you have unburdened yourself of all the debts contained on your list, wrap it in a fancy envelope and tie it with a bow. Write "(your name)'s Mortgage on Happiness and Joy." Go into an open space if possible where you will not be disturbed and burn your "mortgage." As it is consumed by the flames, feel the gratitude for the love and self-trust you have to have had for yourself to finally get rid of this "mortgage" on your joy. Alternatively, gather your friends and family about you, if they are so inclined, and perform the same ritual with them in attendance. Then have a feast of joy in celebration of your freedom from debt. What you all can revel in is the knowledge that the love you share with one another comes gifted from the unconditional source that is your freedom, not from a desperation to control which is your dread.

FAILURE/FAILURE TO BE

Failure is the judgment that we were inadequate to fulfill some task at hand and now we have to be unhappy about that. What is *not* meant here is the simple fact that our efforts often may not bring the results we want. Our inadequacy can stem from two possible sources. One, we simply lack the capacity or capability to attain what we want. Judgements of stupid, inferior, useless, worthless can be applied to ourselves when we experience this. Now whether we actually lack the capability or not is irrelevant, because even when we have the requisite talents, the world may not cooperate with our efforts. But following the logic of "B," we may fault ourselves and fall into self-hatred and despair, the "unbearable wrongness of being me" experience.

Secondly, failure, in the sense we are using it, can be the belief that there is always some way we should have been or could be which would have the power to have gotten us or get us what we want. We just will never be that way, we fear, because we lack the proper motivation to be the way we are supposed to be. Obviously, this is linked to the notion of being bad for ourselves. Even when we want to succeed in a particular enterprise, our fear that we will sabotage our efforts by somehow not doing the right things at the right time can paralyze us and sap our enthusiasm. We then may begin to hate the project that we once loved.

Once a physician, diagnostician of great talent came to me because he had become frozen with fear that he would make the wrong diagnosis. His reputation was solid, with a history of correct judgments about people's problems, but because he had made a minor error in a case recently, he had begun to doubt his capabilities in general. He had bought into the notion that a great burden was on his shoulders to be somehow perfect in all his efforts to make the correct call on all the many and varied physical problems that were presented to him. He certainly did want to be the very best diagnostician he could be, and he had chosen this work with great enthusiasm years before, but now every day was an agony of doubt and terror that he would fail, that something would escape his notice. Naturally, the more frightened he became, the more he fulfilled the basic root meaning of the word "anxiety," which is to "make narrow or to confine." The more anxious he became, the more he lost touch with the ease, freedom and joy of knowing that was exactly what made him such a great physician in the first place. Fortunately, he was able to come to see that his beliefs about having to control the world by being infallible were just what stood in the way of his full expression of his talents. This put him on the road to restoring his confidence and living his joy even in the face of understanding that the complexities of a particular patient's problem might exceed his grasp at times.

So, that is what we fear when we fear that we will fail. More fundamentally, what we are striving to achieve, no matter what it may be—love, financial success, prominence among our fellow humans, mastery of some particular skills, etc.—simply falls under the heading of things that we want. Our failure to achieve them is actually experienced as a failure to do what is necessary in order for us to have permission to be happy, again, in accord with the logic of "B" of those ever-loving ABC's (could be a rock group, no?). Naturally enough then, by understanding failure that way, we dread not being able to fulfill our desires. Further, because our fear can become intense, we begin to find our desires actually burdensome and painful because failure always looms as a judgment ready to fall on us should we falter. This kind of unhappy logic can bring us to hate our goals and to lose interest in them, often through depression, as a way of ridding ourselves of the overwhelming anxiety that can accompany our attempts to fulfill them. Thus something that may have started out as a joyful enterprise can become a nightmare when we follow the twisted logic of becoming unhappy in order to motivate us to get what we want.

Understanding this can free up enormous resources of verve and energy to pursue our desires without regret or constraints. As we will see in Part Two on *Happiness*, this is the true path of prosperity and success.

FAILURE TO BE!

Let us look at this notion of "failure" from an even more fundamental perspective. One of the mistakes people who are just learning Option make is that they take the perfectionist assumptions that are part of the belief structures they have adapted from their experience of culture/society and they overlay those demands upon this new, for them, notion of the Option Method. So, they may experience moments of real breakthrough and joy with all the accompanying euphoria and intensity that may well likely be a part of that. Then as they move through the moments of their lives, they may forget their happiness and find themselves acting and behaving in ways that reflect their life long beliefs in unhappiness in some dimension or other.

This can be the occasion for them to begin to doubt the validity of what they experienced using the Method. Being unhappy is still the dominant way of feeling for them; but they had hoped that they would somehow be beyond unhappiness especially in the light of what may have been such a sense of reality and relief in letting go of some beliefs they had held. Now it seems to them they have failed to maintain that happiness, they have failed to be a way, in the language of their unhappy mode of being, that they were supposed to be. In this case they think they "should have been" happy but they failed to do so. Now they believe that they cannot trust themselves. Perhaps they were fooling themselves. Of course, they are just applying the logic of their beliefs in unhappiness but many will walk away from Option at this juncture because it failed to deliver what it was supposed to in their view.

All that is going on is the belief that there is a way that one is supposed to be as opposed to knowing that there is no way that you can fail to **BE**! All that we are talking about is the fundamental understanding that Being, Freedom and Happiness are the same thing. No one can ever fail to BE, however ludicrous that may sound; that is the first fundamental truth of being and being aware that you *are*. No matter what you may fail to be in the realm of the world, of "B" of the "ABC's", you can never simply fail to BE! And that ground state is sufficient to cover all cases of experience in life as it pertains to your ability to take up an Attitude toward whatever any given moment may present to you. Whether you engage the moment by affirming your happiness or whether you follow the well worn grove of some assumption about how you have to be unhappy about what is presented, you are never in danger of failing to BE, though you may forever fail to be something that you desire to be in world. Over the latter, as we have repeatedly stressed, you have no certainty or control; over the former you have the unalterable and inalienable control of what it means to be a self, a person, a here and now manifestation of being/freedom/happiness.

Keeping this in your mind at each moment will be of enormous practical value in aiding you to build the ongoing Attitude that will make your affirmation of your happiness more and more the likely way you will engage each moment of your existence.

QUESTIONS

- Do you think you have to threaten yourself with unhappiness in the form of fear of failure should you not succeed in getting what you want? Do you think that you would be insufficiently motivated without that fear operating in you?

- How many paths in life did you not take because you feared yourself inadequate to fulfill your goals? How did this fear of failure operate for you then and now?

EXPER/CISES

- Review your life in terms of all the things you have striven to achieve from early childhood. See in what way your original joy and creativity may have been sapped by the fear of not being able to fulfill what you wanted. Now look at what you may be wanting at the moment. See the degree to which you can free your present goals of any fear of failure by using the Method.

DEPRESSION AND DESPAIR

Depression is the belief, held with varying degrees of intensity, that your efforts to be happy are useless, that avenues to joy that you wanted opened up are insolubly thwarted by the non-cooperation of the world with your wants and desires. The refrain from Gilbert and Sullivan that opened this section holds particularly true here, i.e., "The world is but a broken toy, /Its pleasures hollow, false its joy,/ Its pains alone are true…" Despair holds the same relationship to depression that rage holds to anger. It is a more severe instance of depression that tends to be more all-encompassing and fully engaging of your attention, energy and awareness. Depression creates a flattened emotional landscape with tones of gray, but it usually allows a smattering of different colors to peek through in the form of emotional neutrality if not enjoyment. Despair, however, turns the entire universe of self-experience into the darkest apocalyptic tones with little or no respite. It is an acute experience, whereas depression is the chronic version. They both support the 17th century English philosopher

Hobbe's appraisal of life as "nasty, brutish and short," with the only good news being that it's "short!"

The full "logic" of "B" and the consequences of failing to control the world, when such control is believed necessary for your happiness, comes to bear in these states. That is because they represent motivational strategies gone awry, that is, the *failure* of other forms of unhappiness to "work" by somehow helping the person to have sufficient permission, within the allowable cultural/societal variations, to be happy at times. Depression, and more acutely, despair, are acknowledged even by cultural standards as undesirable states, as failures on the part of society to modulate an individual's emotional ranges and create for that person more favorable motivational outcomes through the use of lesser forms of unhappiness. Many times, the depressed or despairing person will reject the ameliorative interventions of family, friends and professionals. The latter are the standard bearers of cultural norms, at least in the West, where the priests and shamans of formal religions have lost a good deal of their authority in trying to normalize people's emotional responses and to carry out the cultural work of moderating what all believe and acknowledge as the inevitable impact of unhappiness on humans.

But the problem here is that often the depressed or despairing person will see through the flaws in the logic that culture is presenting to him or her which basically say that the traditions and mores of the culture will dictate when it is appropriate to be happy and when unhappy. Strange as it may seem, at that point, depressed people are closer to the truth than most others. By following the logic of unhappiness to its natural conclusion, they have decided that they will never get all of what they want, or perhaps in their special instance, some very particular thing that they have decided they require for their happiness. Additionally, if all or part of their depression and despair is based on the *"empathy"* postulate supported by most cultures, then they may feel the failure of culture's control of unhappiness all the more intensely. The *"empathy"* postulate asserts that it ***is not okay to feel happy when there are others in the world who are currently not*** *happy.* We have seen that unhappiness is utilized as a sign of our caring and "goodness" (more on this in the next section). Not to demonstrate our community of caring through, at a minimum, appropriate declarations of outrage, sadness, disappointment, or horror, if not actual felt experiences of the same, would mark us out as unfeeling, uncaring and emotionally alien creatures. On the other hand, to show our loving and caring through all the rituals of affection and actual helpful behaviors in the absence of these empathic experiences of personal discomfort, counts for little or nothing to many.

An experience I had with a person in one of my seminars some years ago captures the essence of the *"empathy"* postulate quite well. She had protested that she could not feel happy in particular instances, despite her declarations that she was a fairly happy person most of the time, when she knew that people were suffering or unhappy about their circumstances. She really meant that in a limited way pertaining mostly to local circumstances about which she had knowledge. I offered her the following scenario (I will call her "Linda" because it blends with "logic" so well to form *"Linda logic"* though I must admit I was tempted to call it *"Aunt Rose logic."* Same thing only with a little garlic and oregano.): "Well, Linda, if you can't allow yourself happiness when there is unhappiness around you, then whenever can you possibly be happy, since unhappiness is an ongoing event for people 24 hours a day around the world? According to your logic, you would never have the right to be happy under the circumstances that now prevail, and have prevailed for all of history as far as we know it."

In other words, I asked her to understand that the logic of her choice to be unhappy in response to the unhappiness of others would require her own ongoing misery every moment of her life. It was totally arbitrary of her to cut off her being unhappy at some point and allow joy to break through. This would be, in the parlance of contemporary psychology, to be in "denial," a place of deficit that would mark her out as someone who was not being the way she should be. By stretching the distorted logic of unhappiness to its extreme this way, it was helpful to her to open herself up to question whether unhappiness was really ever required in order to demonstrate a caring, loving posture towards others. It also tends to break the crust of cultural pretending about how declarations of unhappiness over the misfortune of others counts as an effective way of caring. I mean you weren't really upset about poor Mrs. Thistlewood's pet worm, Freddy, remember? You didn't even attend the funeral did you, you cad?

It opens us to the light of knowing that we are willing to do about the unhappiness or difficulties of others *whatever practically that we are willing to do*. Our **actions** do speak louder than our *declarations of empathy*, no matter how they may be accompanied with personal pain. Such personal experiences do not bring food to the hungry or succor the sick and dying. In any event, we could know what we want for others out of our joy and happiness and act effectively on that knowledge if that is what we choose to do. Unhappiness, as formulated in the *"empathy postulate"* through *"Linda logic,"* is simply irrelevant.

However, for the depressed and despairing, the full weight of *"Linda logic"* falls heavily upon their lives. They have lost the ability to mete out doses of happiness and unhappiness according to some cultural formula. They find no outlet in "denial" but are drawn by the gravity of their miseries to the icy, bottom of a Dante's hell, bereft of hope and even emotional intensities of any kind. This is the "unbearable wrongness of being me" experience at work again. They are perhaps, though, **closer** to the truth about their joy than so many others not so sorely afflicted. The very extremity of their logic about the bleakness of life in the world makes their system of believing quite brittle. Letting go of that logic and its consequences can offer them immediate access to their bliss if they are willing to undertake the Joywork involved.

Lastly, a word about depression and the confusing of physical symptoms with the actual beliefs in unhappiness. People can suffer from a variety of physical illnesses that can mimic depression. Because one doesn't sleep well, or has no energy, or feels listless and lethargic etc., it does not always by any means qualify as depression according to the definition I gave at the outset. However, when people suffer physical complaints in a chronic way, they can then draw conclusions about life which will amount to their being unhappy about feeling so lousy physically. Sometimes merely coming to know that one doesn't have to be unhappy about feeling physically lousy is enough to allow the person to know their happiness even in the presence of physical discomfort. Often when the complaints are addressed holistically, their health and vitality return and they realize that depression was not the primary underlying cause of their physical difficulties, though being unhappy about that certainly can add to their already existing discomforts.

QUESTIONS

- Do you think it would mean anything about you were you not to be unhappy about the misfortunes of others? Remember, no one is asking you to be *happy* about things in the world that you do not have any affection or like for in any way. Rather, the question asks whether you have to be *unhappy* about what happens in the world at any time? Think carefully about that distinction and explore your responses in writing.
- Would you require the pain and unhappiness of others as a sign of their caring of you?
- *Do you want your happiness?* Reach down and pull up the answer. It really is there for you. Act on this!

EXPER/CISES

- Write out a priority list for yourself. Is happiness at the top of the list? If it is not, that will tell you immediately the circumstances under which you will become unhappy. Whatever is at the top of the list ahead of your happiness you have endowed with the power to make you unhappy if it is not acquired or fulfilled. Examine what there is about anything like that that would supersede your happiness using the Method and the understandings gleaned from what you know at this point.

DEATH AND LOSS

Death, whether it be of another or of oneself, brings up the same belief. It is a variant of not getting what you want. In the first instance, the loss of another, it means that you will not have that person available for the reasons that you want them available and that means you will not get what you want. In the second instance, it means that you will lose the most profound object of your love and concern, yourself. You will not be available to yourself. You will not be getting what you want. It is the ultimate victory of "B" of the ABC's over you in that your not controlling the world literally deprives you of your life whether you want that to happen or not. As with all instances of unhappiness, the belief that not getting what you want requires unhappiness is also at the root of why we would become unhappy around the issue of death.

Additionally, there is the cultural imperative, found in most societies, that the loss of another requires the expression of unhappiness in the form of sadness or grief. Here we are dealing with a motivational issue once more. Presumably we mourn the loss of another out of love for them. Certainly, when someone we do not like dies, there is little incentive to demonstrate mourning, even though we may want to show some concern if only in a formal, perfunctory manner (remember Freddy!). So it is not death itself that prompts such a response, but rather the death of those whom we have endowed with some meaning through our love. Now if love for another would prompt unhappiness in the form of mourning, then we can certainly ask why.

Do we mourn or rejoice at the birth of our children? The love we feel is created by us freely for the new child. There is no pain or dread in this love, unless we place it there by limiting our love through our beliefs in unhappiness. As we care for and nurture those we love, what is our motive? We have just read the section on Owing and could now know that our love does not have to have any trace of that form of unhappiness to it in order for us to be motivated to do for another what we want to do out of our love. So, what could our grief and sadness possibly mean? From the point of view of society and cultural norms, do we believe that not to show unhappiness at the death of a loved one would prove that we really did not love them?

We are told by contemporary experts in psychology, that mourning is a necessary process and not to engage in it is actually bad for our mental health. But isn't this just another case of exalting some form of unhappiness as a way of compensating us for undergoing it? Isn't it just another case of how it is actually good to feel bad, so that then we have permission to feel good again? So, there may be a number of unhappy assumptions operating around the issue of death and loss, but they all amount to the fear that there would be something wrong with us were we not to demonstrate the requisite fears and sadness. That without those feelings, we could not lay claim to truly loving anyone. Being motivated by our joy in experiencing the other person in our lives is insufficient. We must pay the price of pain in order to pass the test of having true love. So love becomes encumbered with the promise of pain in loss. It is no wonder that people are reticent to manifest their love when such a feeling state would ultimately have to end in anguish. Despite the propaganda that grief is a wonderful thing, and good for us, we all recognize it for what it is, pain and unhappiness.

There is an "Aunt Rose" tale I tell about how she reacted to the death of my father, who was her brother. To be sure, she was "appropriately" upset but in a quiet sort of way prior to showing up at the wake. When she arrived, I went to escort her up to the casket where my father was laid out according to custom. She entered the room, a veritable mountain of Sicilian black lace. In the front row to the right sat a contingent of the *dona* and the *nona,* the local Italian ladies of venerable age dressed in black, some with gold teeth. They saw her. She saw them. The transformation put Kafka's "Metamorphosis" to shame. From an upright, stable, mobile, fleshy cathedral, she threw herself on the floor and instantly became a sort of giant Italian beetle, rolling and writhing in loud moans and exclamations of grief while tearing at her Sicilian lace (not tearing too hard to do too much damage, I noted). I was left standing there with my mouth agape wondering for a moment what was going on until it instantly became obvious. She was going through her mourning routine, *a la Siciliana.* In this cultural dispensation, one doesn't approach the body of one's dead brother like some WASP and merely dab a careful tear or two from one's eyes. Oh no! This had to be a Mediterranean production worthy of "*Medea.*"

By now we could know that we don't have to buy into such myths. We certainly don't have to like or accept the death of those we love. I in no way wanted the deaths of my father and mother. But in addition to losing them as real time companions in my joy, did I have to feel emotional pain? No. My loving them was a solid knowledge. If there were tears, they were tears of gratitude for what I had received by knowing them. The Option Method is the wonderful liberating way to move beyond tears of sadness and grief to tears of gratitude and joy for having had those we love in our lives. Without the grief, we can have ready access to our memory of them and revel in the ongoing sense of their presence as a treasured gift in our lives. Of course, as with all categories of unhappiness, it is never wrong or bad, nor could there ever be any judgment about being unhappy. Of course not. Rather, I am here to offer what I consider the true alternative to such beliefs: your joy and your happiness as the wellsprings of your love for yourself and others.

QUESTIONS

- Do you in any way feel that not to experience grief over the loss of a loved one would mean you were a heartless, unloving individual?
- Do you have any fears of your own death? Examine them in very specific terms using the Method.

EXPER/CISES

- Fear of death focuses on some hypothetical time when you will not be available to yourself, and somehow you will know that you are not available to yourself and be unhappy about that. Reread the section on *Time* and learn to understand that you will always be available to yourself for as long as there is a self for you to be available to. That will always be "now." Getting rid of a misunderstanding of time will help to dissipate any sense that you will be made unhappy by some impossible situation, i.e., that there is no longer any "you" and somehow "you" are aware of this and made unhappy by that knowledge. That is just your here and now dread of there not being a "you" in the future.
- Do the first "exper/cise" in the section on *Anger/Rage/Liking and Not Liking*. It will be very appropriate to your understanding of what we have been saying in this section.

CHAPTER SIX

HAPPINESS

HAPPINESS

Ecclesiastes 3:12
I know for sure that there is absolutely
nothing better for them than being happy and
making the best life for themselves.
Translation from the Hebrew by Bruce Di Marsico

We have examined a wide range of beliefs in unhappiness and hopefully you have made some real progress is letting go of many of them. It was necessary to review these views on unhappiness in order to clear a path for a discussion of happiness and some of its attributes. Again, this discussion will hardly be exhaustive, since being happy has endless possibilities. This is just a small taste to prime the pump of your own Joybuilding activities and discoveries. In the last section, we dealt primarily with the logic of "B" of the ABC's. Now we will be more focused on "C" and what it holds for us. Remember:

A: There is just you and the world
B: You don't control the world
C: You do control the attitude you construct toward whatever the world presents to you each moment of your existence.

FREEDOM TO BE DIFFERENT, I.E., WHO YOU ARE.

Certainly one of the great joys of knowing the truth about your happiness is the wonderful freedom that can follow for you to be whoever you want to be. I literally mean that you make yourself up attitudinally in all the postures you take towards life and living. You don't make up the universe and its laws of course, but that is not what you want anyway. What you want is your happiness. Once you know that happiness is secure for you by virtue of your *being* your happiness and your freedom, then all questions of how you are to be are basically your own. Of course, you are limited by the laws of physics and by the constraints of the time and place you occupy in history, the social contexts etc. But, since you are not constrained by any inner drive to have to be any particular way to be happy, you are quite free to make yourself up within the giveness of the contexts just described. Being the sole author of your emotions, of your attitudinal destiny, you can give way to the creative verve to become whatever it is you find interesting to become. Of course, there is no guarantee that the world will accept how you make yourself up, but no matter. If one version doesn't work, why not try another? You will more than likely want to avoid undesirable consequences that might occur as part of who you decide to be. So undoubtedly you will put into the colors of your creative palette whatever understandings of the boundaries and covenants of your cultural world you believe will help to avoid such consequences.

Without any fear of failure or fear that others have the power to deprive you of your happiness, you can approach each moment of your existence with a prudent but real sense of fearlessness. Without any sense of being afraid of rejection or of being made a fool of, you can engage people with boldness and passionate intensity. Why not? Nothing is at stake. You know the world is your playground. That is exactly why you are here, to play and to enjoy the fruits and pleasures that come from such creative play. Others may not posses this knowledge and they may treat the world in somber, apocalyptic terms that make it seem to them more a killing field than a playground. This is simply their believing whatever it is they believe and living out the consequences of that belief. They are still doing the best they know to do given what they believe, so you are not burdened with judging them; however you might want to keep out of their way, given what they may believe and the narrow and dread -driven way they interpret what is licit in life.

The implications of this freedom are vast. We have reviewed in the previous sections (Section 8, *The Dread of Not Getting What We Want* as just one example) just how much dread humans experience in the face of their freedom. Thus, it may take a little getting used to before you give fuller rein to your authorial autonomy. That's fine too. You will play more freely as over time you discover more and more the truth of what is being said here. In the meanwhile, enjoy your explorations. I know I have enjoyed mine. And yes, I did find this freedom to be threatening initially, indeed as it had been all of my life until I came upon this perspective. But gradually over time by doing what I now call my Joywork I have come to see this freedom as the twin brother to my happiness. And yet, to most, I am a fairly conventional person. Finding ways to navigate through, around and with the conventions and covenants that define this time, place and cultural setting is not a chore, but part of finding the best possible ways to play in the world within the allowable limits. Remember, the primary way of being "different" is to affirm and live your happiness each moment. As I move from moment to moment, that sense of difference comes alive both in the contrast from what I recall my moment to moment existence to have been, and the often exquisite way the world opens up to my explorations of it through my capacity to notice nuances that I was formerly blind to by virtue of my unhappiness. So, like Aunt Rose's exhortations at dinner time (always the best time in that house) to "dig in," go ahead and do just that. Dig into the feast of life and flesh your teeth on the joyous food of existence!

QUESTIONS

- Do you see yourself as somehow pigeonholed by how you have been in your past? Do you feel that how you have been must necessarily limit what you might desire as goals for yourself right now? Answer these questions using what you now have come to know.
- Is there anything about you holding the author's pen of your own life in your own hands that you resist? Do you in any way fear the freedom you have to create yourself? Do you believe such freedom would actually cause you somehow to become unhappy?

EXPER/CISES

- Sit down and write out your most outrageous visions of yourself. Use the spirit of the "Happy Nut" resident in all of us. It helps if 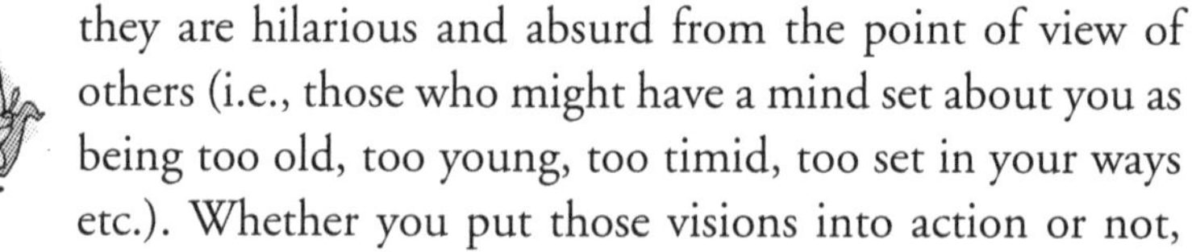 they are hilarious and absurd from the point of view of others (i.e., those who might have a mind set about you as being too old, too young, too timid, too set in your ways etc.). Whether you put those visions into action or not, see if there is any resistance to your freedom to act on them if you so chose. If you have friends who also are coming to know the truth about their happiness, this can be a group exper/cise. Everyone can come as to a costume party, dressed as or acting as the character or person they would like to become. Friendly jibes and general frolicking will bring out the ham in all of us. Enjoy!

- Experiment with trying new directions more in accordance with your revised understanding of what you would like for yourself. Make note of all your responses and deal with any unhappiness that you might discover as you expand your world.

FREEDOM TO WANT/ THE ROOTS OF PROSPERITY AND SUCCESS

As with unhappiness, all the streams of happiness flow from the same source: our being in the world as free and happy entities. Therefore, all the freedoms we will explore and all the categories of happiness we will briefly examine will have echoes of each other as we look at their potentials for us.

The freedom to want is an essential understanding of how we actualize our happiness in the concrete circumstances of each moment. Our cultural upbringing and subsequent beliefs in unhappiness have led to our being hesitant, constrained and troubled over our wants. One main aspect of that is demonstrated when we see how wanting our happiness is portrayed as something not to trust; how our freedom to want might lead us to be ways we are not supposed to be, and ultimately to the state of the unbearable wrongness of being ourselves, to evil. (A review of Section 7and 9 will help here.) The second main aspect comes from our having allowed ourselves to believe that mere wanting is an insufficient motivation for getting what we want, so that we introduce the concept of needs to heighten our sense of urgency around getting what we want. (Section 9 will also help here.) All these conceits have collapsed like a house of cards before the refreshing breeze of our true freedom to want whatever we might want, without restraints or caveats of any kind.

We can do so because our wanting is the cutting edge of our creative engagement with the world. Without any dread-driven sense that we must have what we want in order to be happy, we are totally free to throw the dice of our wants onto the crap table of each unfolding moment ruled by the laws of uncertainty and incompleteness. Sometimes we will find we "win" while, sometimes, perhaps more often than not, we will "lose." But what is not at stake in this playing in the world is precisely what we want most of all (and, wonder of wonders, what we possess before we enter into the playground of life), that is, our happiness.

So, do you see? Our freedom to be different is connected to our freedom to want whatever we might want. Being comfortable with our wants allows us to explore more of the world and out of that exploration to discover ways of being that we may apply to ourselves. You might want to take a trip to the Tuscany region of Italy, and after eating your way through the hill towns discover that you would like to distinguish yourself as a fine cook! Wanting and Being different work hand in hand to generate innovation and uniqueness, traits that can be very attractive in presenting products to a world jaded by the intensities of media blitzing.

As we can now see, when we stop burdening our wanting with needs and dread of failure because the world will not cooperate with our attempts to make it what we want it to be, then paradoxically, we can achieve a clarity about not only what we want but how we will go about getting it. This clarity is unlikely to exist in the anxiety-filled atmosphere of our former unhappy beliefs. There are many examples in my book *Joywords* and on my audio tapes. Still another one that comes to mind is a young man who sought help because he could not please his superior at work in a large blue chip corporation. The superior demanded he work extremely long hours and on the weekends, a demand that put a good deal of pressure on his still young marriage of just a few years. He was in a deep quandary because no matter how he tried to produce results, his boss was not satisfied. He felt what he described as an *absolute need* to excel and to do so he had to control the world in the form of his boss by producing material results that would bring about that effect.

Having failed at this, he was falling into a depression. (No matter what he did he could not control some aspect of the world. The old "B" logic at work.) He described dreams where he was attempting to crawl out of a bottomless hole whose sides became increasingly slippery as he approached the surface, so he was losing his grip. Dread seized him as he saw his control strategies fail. His wife threatened to leave him and that brought him to seek some help. Through the Option dialogues, he began to open up to a new perspective. Once he was able to surrender his commitment to the control logic of "B" of the ABC's, he began to consider the options available in the realm of "C." He decided that, while he did want to be successful, he wanted his happiness most of all, because this was in fact what success meant to him in the first place. Once he began to see that he had his happiness no matter what the outcome of his attempts to excel in his career, he took a whole new different approach. He quit his job and began a home-based consultation service. At first it was touch and go, but gradually as he became happier, he found that he had much greater access to his own creative talents. This paid off in the acquisition of customers that in relatively short time assured the success of his venture. All this was done in a time commitment that left plenty of space for his new family.

This is the root of prosperity and success from an Option point of view. I do not speak of somehow manipulating the universe through the magic of being some special way you are supposed to be so that the world will somehow be forced thereby to cough up whatever it is you want. No, that is mere conjuring and illusion. What I mean is that once you know you have what you want most of all out of your existence, your happiness, secure in the bosom of your own being, then life truly becomes play. It becomes play that is lived out of total comfort, without dread or angst about how things will turn out. You know you will apply your creative intelligence and muster whatever resources you have to enter the game in the best way you know how. It does not guarantee some magical outcome, but it does mean that you will be utilizing all of yourself optimally to gain success. Does it not stand to reason that with such clarity and sense of ease in strategizing about how best to achieve your goals, you have created the most advantageous environment to maximize the likelihood that they will indeed be achieved? Keep in mind as well that your joy is in all aspects of what you do. It is in the planning of it, the carrying out of the plans and in the outcome, whatever it might be. You don't have to wait and withhold your joy until you find out whether the world will cooperate with your attempts. Your happiness is always now, so again you are free to be as bold and innovative as your creative self can contrive to be.

QUESTIONS

- Do you have any sense that it is illegitimate to give free rein to your wanting? Is there any sense of dread about being so free? Think of things in your immediate life experience that you may be frightened of because they would require a greater freedom than you have been used to allowing for yourself.
- Do you feel that there is some special way you have to be in order to "merit" success in the world? Do you equate success with happiness?

EXER/CISES

- Take out a photograph album of yourself from the earliest age you have photos. If this is not available, simply take time to recall yourself from your earliest memories up to the present. As you go over each picture or memory, try to recall what you wanted at the time. Write it down. When you have completed your historical review, look over what you wanted. What sense do you have about how you felt in wanting those things in the past? If there is any sense now that your wanting was not legitimate, question your feelings using the Method. After the review, focus on your present wants. Do you notice that what you want has changed and is changing in the light of your willingness to give free rein to your wanting? Make note of the changes. See how comfortable you are with them.

FREEDOM FROM BLAME/ INNOCENCE REGAINED

In the section on *Doing the Best we Know To Do*, the point was made that we operate from moment to moment, in each unfolding instant, according to our beliefs. We are free to exercise our beliefs, free to be happy or unhappy, but once the moment is past, then it represents information and nothing else. There is no way that that information, no matter what it is, can deprive us of experiencing our happiness now, in this moment. We have done whatever we have done to gain our happiness or to avoid the greater unhappiness. We may have been very unhappy in doing whatever we have done. There may be consequences to us for our actions coming from others. They may have found themselves affected by our actions and now want to bring those consequences to bear as a means of compensating themselves or society for whatever they feel we may have done that warrants such compensation. It may be in the form of money, goods, our personal freedom for specified lengths of time, or even our life.

That is responsibility and it represents an important part of the laws and covenants of any social grouping. We may agree or disagree with elements of those social agreements, but we may also find ourselves experiencing the consequences of violating them. None of this has to involve blame, judgment or hatred. We may even, from the perspective of being happy right now, not object to the consequences meted out for how we have been because we value the importance of maintaining social order and no longer agree with or value the behavior for which we are now subject to consequences. We could also know that living out of our happiness in this moment makes it most unlikely that we would ever trespass on the physical integrity of another person, or deprive them of property or rights due them by the agreements and covenants of this time and place in history. There is no motivation driven by any form of misery to fuel such behaviors. Just think of what we discussed in Section 10, *Fear of Being Bad For Ourselves*, and review the examples given there. Those examples should help to underline the point we are making that without the pressure of believing in "needs" or "urges" which must be satisfied in order to be happy, there is no real incentive to harm or impede the freedom of others. There may be all sorts of pragmatic entanglements and disagreements to settle, but without the burden of unhappiness to cloud issues, the chances for harmonious resolutions surely are greater.

The most important point here is that each moment is absolutely a whole new birth of possibilities, an entire universe exploding into being for us to enjoy. Our behaviors and beliefs prior to this moment represent how we have been up to *now*. In each unfolding moment there is spread out before us an unlimited potential to be completely different, to experience our joy and felicity without limit. In that moment we can fulfill a prime meaning of the word **"innocence"** which is *not to know evil*. Indeed, if we discover our happiness in this moment, we will by doing so also discover that "evil" is just a word to describe the greatest unhappiness we can fear in others and in ourselves. Since by knowing our happiness we know that there is no unhappiness, we can truly say for ourselves, that we have no knowledge of evil, hence *we are innocent.*

QUESTIONS

- Does the notion that you are "innocent" cause you discomfort? Do you want to object and confess some aspect of yourself or past experience as making innocence impossible?
- When will you be free and innocent? When all around you are happy and well? When all the problems of the world are solved to your satisfaction? When everyone else acknowledges you to be free and innocent?

EXPER/CISES

- Again, review your whole life from your earliest moments to the present using whatever items that may best prompt your memory. When did you lose your "innocence"? See how coming to know about good and bad and evil became the moments when you lost touch with yourself as innocent in each moment. Make note of how many objections remain to your declaring your innocence. For each instance find a small rock or pebble and put it in a bag or sack. When you can, take a walk in your favorite quiet place. Breath comfortably and deeply. Sense the abundance of good will you have for yourself as you accept your innocence in this moment. Embrace yourself (or others, should you be doing this as a group exper/cise) and enjoy the feeling of openness in your body as you come alive to the truth of your joy. Take each rock, one at a time, and toss it away, over a cliff, into a lake, or just as far away as you can manage. The weight of your unhappiness can be carried aloft with the rocks and render you as light and free as your own breath.
- Imagine this day, this moment, this instant to be the actual moment of your birth and here you are born full grown and filled with the knowledge of your happiness. Step forward into this moment with as total a feeling of innocence and freedom from any hint or burden of unhappiness as possible. Breathe in the wonder that can accompany that movement. Live in it and record what it was like for you when you can.

FREEDOM TO LOVE

Love is the spontaneous fruit of being free and happy. It is born in that matrix of endless generativity that is your joy. It cannot be demanded of you by another out of obligation or intimidation. It is not given because people are "deserving" or "not deserving." There are no predictable limits to love. It cannot be captured or constrained by the demands of culture or anyone else no matter what their alleged claim on our love may be. That is precisely why love is so highly prized above all other things. It is also why it can only truly thrive in an atmosphere of freedom. Fear and unhappiness of any kind will limit and discourage love from occurring in us or in others. The fact that it is an attribute of freedom and joy paradoxically makes loving an ongoing problem for those who are unhappy. Since the hallmark of unhappiness is the fear of not getting what we want, then when that attitude is turned toward love, it is easy to see how one can easily quench the flame of love by attempting to grasp it and make it a prisoner of our requirement for certainty. We have said so many times that the world and those who populate it do not always cooperate with our values, with our wants and desires. If we make love an object of need and necessity, we are setting up precisely the environment of unhappiness where it is least likely to thrive and most likely to be smothered by our demands that the loved ones be the way we say they have to be in order for us to be happy.

When you remove unhappiness from the equation of loving, ah, then a whole new dimension opens up to you. Now loving comes to be what I described it to be: the spontaneous outpouring of affirmation and behaviors towards another person *for no reason*! Yes, that is right, for no reason. Though we may enumerate the qualities about another which interest us and draw us into closer contact, yet none of those qualities, beauty, intelligence, warmth, etc., have any power to "make" us love anyone. Our love is a deep reflection of the divine within us. ***That is, it is given not for cause, but for the freely willed joy of doing so.*** Here is the wonder of love. If love were merely a commodity to be exchanged it would be more a commercial investment. If other people's qualities had some magical power to make us in love, against our wills, then love would be a form of unhappiness.

Do you see? You can pile reason upon reason why you should love someone. I remember my Aunt Rose trying to fix me up with some suitable Italian, Sicilian girl. She went through all the charms, like the ability to make *pasta con sarde* with just the right bucatini pasta and the right blend of sardines and *fenuchio* (fennel). She pointed to the configuration of the hips which meant that many bambinos could be created with no problem. *Qualche fusto!*(What a body!) Then there was the dedication to church going and so forth. Well, what can I say? Somehow, chowhound though I am, these qualities did not add up to love. Yes, yes, I know, when you begin to "fall in love" you wax eloquent about the virtues of the beloved, the physical attributes, the intelligence, the compassion etc. But those very attributes often alter and fade over time while the decision to love can remain. How so? I assert it is because the decision to love is independent of those attributes and thus can survive alterations, i.e. "love is not love/ which alters when it alteration finds." You begin to get the picture, right?

Now that does **not** mean that love does not request the beloved to be certain ways. We can want whatever we want out of those preferences. We can also love with little or no request that the other be any certain way for us. That is completely up to us. ***Our love is completely a gift of our freedom.*** In that sense of being causeless, i.e., not subject to the demands or expectations of another, it can be extended to another no matter what their response to it. They can spit on it, reject it out of hand, or embrace it with boundless gratitude. Anyone who has raised children through their teen years will attest to this. We will love whom we wish how we wish, with or without any requirements for another to be a certain way or even reciprocate. Such is our freedom to love.

What I want to make clear is that the unconditional nature of love refers only to the fact that it is a product of our freedom. Love may often have conditions and preferences. You may require that the one you love does not use physical violence against you or those you cherish. You may require your lover to be honest with you. You may want a monogamous relationship. You may prefer someone who doesn't use alcohol or drugs, wants children, loves animals, takes a shower every day, is not a communist or fascist or fundamentalist ideologue—the list is open ended and purely up to you. Of course each requirement or preference has the consequence of limiting your choices. But so what. You are free to want what you want. Whether the world cooperates by giving it to you—that, as we have seen throughout this book, is quite another matter. But, your happiness doesn't depend on that cooperation. Now just as our freedom to be happy cannot be conditioned by any power the world or people exercise, so too our love shares in the same unconditionality. Just as we cannot be made to be a way we don't want to be against our wills (I am talking now of course about our happiness only, remember) so too we cannot be made to love someone against our wills. For me, unconditional does not mean that our love is somehow diminished by our freedom also to want those we love to relate to us in ways we prefer and not in other ways. They may not honor that and we may still love them, but our wanting is not in conflict with the unconditional nature of love as I have just described it.

To repeat, then, our freedom to be happy is unconditional and unconditioned by anything and therefore our loving shares in that form of unconditionality. However, again, we are precisely free to love or not love for no reason, meaning again that nothing constrains our freedom to be attitudinally the way that we want to be. We will decide on the basis of what seems good for us whether we will continue to love or not. That is what makes love problematic, as mentioned earlier, for those who are unhappy because of their inability to tolerate living in the uncertainty that freedom truly represents. *However, when we know that the love of others given or withheld has no power to deprive us of our happiness*, then loving becomes, like wanting, the wonder of playing in the world with those who wish to join us in our play. That can be for a moment or a lifetime, but however long it may last, love is given, as happiness is experienced, one moment at a time.

That is how I experience loving those close to me. There is not always a meeting of the minds about how we relate to one another. There are times when their preferences or mine are not fulfilled. Thus far, through all the tumultuousness of family life and its politics, love has remained, changed and in many respects grown deeper. What the future holds, I do not know, but I can speak for the love that exists as I write these words. Perhaps my experience with my dogs is illustrative as well. They have been great teachers of patience and constancy. By not judging them and loving them with great gusto, I have gotten back a verve and intensity that is available at every instant. They are more nearly creatures of the present because they lack our capacity for carrying around the legacy of their beliefs in unhappiness to color each moment of their lives. This gives them an immediacy, tenderness and joy that adds many dimensions of happiness to the palette of love that exists around me.

Knowing our joy, then, we can enjoy thereby the love others offer us without dread of how it may be offered, what conditions may be placed upon it, or whether it will be constant or withdrawn. We can decide from moment to moment whether what others want of us as partners in love is what we actually want as well. We can do this without fear of rejection or judgment, without blame, rancor or resentment when others do not get what they want from us, or we from them. We are free to love them as we choose and they are free to do the same. We are also free to be as fully revealing to a love partner as we wish. Should their coming to know us become the occasion for their not continuing their love, that can actually be a blessing. Why? Because it frees us up to seek out someone who will be more comfortable with who we are and more enthusiastic about loving us.

We have no reason from unhappiness or fear of rejection to withhold who we are from another. When we come upon someone who comes to know us fully and offers their love without reservation about that knowledge, ah, then, we can rejoice in being truly loved. All of us are living the same truth about our joy and happiness and we are free to create in the time and space available to us in a lifetime whatever arrangements of love, caring, compassion and nurturance we so choose. They are the gifts of our freedom to others and we can exalt in receiving the same gifts from them when they are available.

QUESTIONS

- Do you fear to love because others may not reciprocate or if they do they may not continue to love you?

- I have posited that love is not based on "reasons" to love but on our unconditional freedom to love. To the degree that you can begin to find this a comfortable concept, can you also understand that, since there is no reason for anyone to love you, if they do, particularly in the light of your sharing who you are as fully as you know how, there is essentially nothing about yourself you have to fear will somehow cause your lover to terminate his/her love? Does knowing that incline you more toward opening yourself up to loving?

EXER/CISES

- If you have had the experience of having children, then recall the moment when you decided to love your child. Yes, it may feel like it just arose from nowhere and was magically present, but that is just the point. Here was an experience of that freedom and spontaneity talked about earlier. Contrast this with the instances where you feared loss of love or found yourself not wanting to love. Everyone has had such experiences. Now, examine how you are loving right now. To what degree is your loving tinged with fear or anxiety? Note this and use the Method to free yourself of those unhappy feelings. As you do, find time each day to experiment with loving for the pure joy of loving. As you become more comfortable, decide whether you want to really let those you love know you fully. As you let go of your reservations about openness, note how your happiness grows whether others respond in the ways you wish or not.

- As you become alive to the freedom that love represents, experiment with offering it to larger and larger circles of people. Remember, love will always be specific instances of loving, in specific moments of time. Love will not obligate or constrain you. See the truth of that as you live your love out of greater and greater freedom. Note that as you do, it becomes easier to love, easier to expand the community of your loving with others. Write down your progress in this Joywork.

TO LOVE IS TO BE HAPPY

A writing of Bruce Di Marsico from 1975. This is a wonderful reference from the creator of the Option Method. Keeping this in mind as you work through your beliefs around Love, Relationships and related matters can be a wonderful way to help achieve clarity and increase your happiness. Anyone interested in reading more about Bruce and purchasing tapes and a collection of his writings when they come available can look at: *http://www.optionmethodnetwork.com/tape1.htm* or be in touch with Deborah Di Marsico at *BMDOption@aol.com*.

To love is to be happy and do what you want, whatever you want. Be with. Don't be with. Smile, don't smile. Be loving don't be loving (affectionate). Give or say whatever you want, take or ask for whatever you want. If the one you love gets unhappy, don't believe you are not loving them enough for them to be happy. Their happiness does not depend on you. If you find you want them to be happy it is because you want it; not because you must be a "loving" person to prove to them or you that you can love. You are loving if you are happy (if you know you are not afraid).

If you are happy with someone in order to be a "loving" nice person, then your happiness will depend on seeing them seeing you as loving or your seeing yourself as loving. Every time you don't feel "loving" or giving what they ask of you, or every time they don't act loved or loving and don't give you what you ask—then you will feel like a failure as a lover. It will get to the point that you will be over aware of your failure.

If you are the "failure" by being the guilty, ungiving, unfeeling one, you will need to run away. You will be repulsed by your lover and play right into their fear of failure.

If you are the "failure" by not being able to accept only what is offered to you, by not being able to "get love", you will be over attracted to your lover and play right into their fear of failure.

That kind of view of being a lover is really worth failing at. You only fail to love if you get unhappy. In this relationship you only get unhappy though because you believe you failed to love.

You are not really failing to love if you don't feel or do in such a way that "prevents" your lover from being unhappy. You fail to love by getting unhappy about that. You fail to love if you are afraid of your lover (being unhappy).

If you want evidence that you are a loving person, you will only find it as your happiness. If you are happy, you are loving everyone.

A lover is not someone you are more happy with. A lover is someone you are with happily. When you are happy, you will want more things from and with some people more than others. When you are happy, you will want to give to some people more than others. If a lover is different or special, it is because you are both wanting very much together.

When you are happy, you are glad for everyone's happiness. You may not be aware though that you are especially glad that they are doing what they want. You are happy that they are doing what they want but you are not especially aware that it is for you or exactly what you are wanting (although you may not be aware of wanting them to do anything different).

With a lover you are glad for everything they do that they do when they are happy. You find that if you are not glad, it is because they are not so happy and are not especially doing what they want.

You are aware of any fear in them, any loss of happiness. You know each other perfectly in the sense that you are as aware of their gladness and happiness as you are of your own.

It is not because you are afraid of their unhappiness (although you can be at the point) but because you are wanting them (because you want to, and they want you to) to be happy.

You love them and want their happiness and the gladness you will both have when they are happy. A lover is someone who you want to be glad with together.

Lovers are two people who come together to "learn" how to not be unhappy and who look forward to more gladness. They come together not to learn how to be loving to someone but to grow in happiness.

You want to see happiness and gladness in them and you want them to see (know) those in you. You want to "help" each other have more happiness and less fear. The only way to help is to be happy yourself and do what you want. Don't be unhappy about their unhappiness.

The problems and games set in after one gets unhappy either with themselves or you. They usually experience it as "failing" to love you and resenting your wanting something they are afraid of "failing" at.

It is of course the fear of failing at being loving. They are more concerned with looking loving than being happy. They feel tested by you. They are quick to believe and imagine that they are hurting you by not giving or doing what they believe you want. They do not believe that no matter what you may have wanted, you certainly didn't want them to get unhappy.

The games begin if you believe that you have not been "loving" enough or that you can overcome their unhappiness by being more "loving". In short, you start playing if you believe there is anything happening for you to be unhappy about. Then you will be oh so loving, understanding, forgiving, eager to fix things, showing how loving you are. That will turn them off more and turn you on more. You are now both afraid of being unloving and are both believing that loving is where it's at.

You are now being "loving" in order to get them to love you. You feel you just want them to be happy but you are wanting it so that it will show how loving you can be. You even hope to inspire them to be "loving". You both want to achieve what is the cause of the problem—"Lovingness".

Real love is to be happy and to just want them to be happy (if that is what you truly want). You make your choice: Do you want to be happy and love or be "loving" instead.

The difference between Loving and "loving" is a choice of intention, the behavior may be the same but the motivation is vastly different. You can be loving but it will never be your lover that you love. You will just be loving your lovingness. A lover is someone with whom you don't have to be loving in order to get what you want. You don't even have to be happy to get what you want from them. They have to be happy for you to get what you want from them. You have to be happy only to be what you want to be—happy. Then they will get what they want from you.

When your lover does not accept what you offer that you think they want to have, just let yourself know that you do what you want. You are not unhappy because it seems that you were wrong. If they are not glad for the offer, it is because they are unhappy. You don't want them to take in order to be nice and loving toward you. You want them to be happy. Do not test yourself to see if you are unloving or unhappy.

The unhappy "loving" is being nice when you don't feel like it and doing what you believe is not what you want. The test or split exists because it is obvious that sometimes unhappy people will want "proof" of your lovingness. If you are more concerned with appearing loving, you will either do what they want (without feeling like it) or you will be turned off and refuse even if you really want to do it.

Being happy is something you can do for someone even if they need it as a proof of love, if you want to. You can never know which if you get unhappy about their unhappiness

You are always unhappy every time (or all the time) and for as long as you hold to the belief that you want to get love by being "loving" or you want to return love by feeling loving.

Love is not something you beam at someone like a search-light or gun. It is being happy and knowing that you are naturally loving by doing whatever you want. Knowing that you will give them whatever you want (no more, no less) without fear of not being loving enough.

Do not be concerned if your lover is not "loving". You can know you are happy and love if you can say yes or no freely and if your lover can freely say yes or no to your offers. You love and are happy if you allow another to say no.—If they do not have to accept your gift.

Our real wanting is not to succeed or fail at being lovers or teachers or students or friends, etc.. but just to be happy. I do not fail you if you or I fail to be happy. You do not fail me if you or I are unhappy.

I can be happy because I can be and want to be. You can be happy because you can be and want to be.

GRATITUDE

I find that the most constant vehicle for taking joy in the world is gratitude. Gratitude and happiness mutually amplify one another. Gratitude is the discovery that everything in the world is a potential source of wonder and joy. Whatever the world is, you suddenly become aware that you are the prism with an infinite number of facets to reflect back to yourself whatever portion of reality you may chance upon in a dazzling refraction of elation and happiness. Prior to knowing that, as you cast your eyes about you, what you found were whole areas of experience that were "dead" to you in the sense that they were already prejudged to contain no possibility of joy. As you progress in your understanding of your happiness, you will find that more and more the scales fall from your eyes and you are free to see wonder all about you and take pleasure in that experience. Gratitude is the growing sense that the universe has been rendered a place of meaning and that even more wonderfully, this meaning comes exclusively through you. Yes of course, I know there are many things about the world that you do not like and do not accept, and that is just fine. You can have gratitude for feeling free and comfortable to have your preferences and passions comfortably without concern that they in any way reflect any defect in you. Never in your wildest dreams would you have thought that your deepest wish would be realized, your wish to be the arbiter of meaning for yourself. As the truth of this unfolds, your Gratitude increases. As your Gratitude increases, your capacity to see deeper and broader vistas of potential joy increases. It is a mutually enhancing procedure that knows no bounds. It is limited only by your openness to being grateful for the happiness you have brought yourself by letting go of unhappy beliefs and living your joy in any given moment of your life.

QUESTIONS:

- Is there any feeling at all that if you were to feel grateful in this moment, you would be letting go of some important safeguards or ways of making sure that you will not be taken advantage of, i.e., be out of emotional self-control?
- Is there any sense that your gratitude must await the changes that others/the world must make so that they will be worthy of your gratitude?
- Do feelings of gratitude in any way seem to bring up discomforting or unhappy feelings with them? If so, then let those feelings become explicit and examine them using the Option Method, so that your gratitude won't be diluted with a mixture of sadness or other emotionally painful sensations.

EXPER/CISES:

- Pick something in your environment/life right now whose existence has a history of being meaningful to you (son, daughter, parents, friends, teachers, pets etc.) and allow yourself to build feelings of gratitude for their presence i.e., their being there without any need on your part to control what they are. Let all the reasons for being grateful simply well up and become alive to you. As you feel grateful, allow the gratitude to move slowly beyond the reasons you have given yourself. Let the sense of pure gratitude become the focus of how your feelings are formed. By this I mean that like love, gratitude is essentially causeless. It arises out of a fundamental sense of joy over merely existing and being able to participate in life. I understand that this concept is undoubtedly new to you. So be adventurous and see how you can play with it by coming to it in the best way you know how. Okay? Notice how joyful you become as you resonate to the rhythms of being grateful. Allow the gratitude and the joy to merge into a synergy of wonder and elation. Stay with the experience for as long as you wish. Record your responses.

- Now, pick anything in your environment at this moment that has more minor relevance and usefulness in your life relative to the first instance above (your washing machine, the mailman, the aroma of a particularly flavorful food, some favorite hobby etc.) and simply see what it would be like to be grateful for its existence. Again, as with the earlier example, let the reasons you give yourself for your gratitude become as explicit as you seem to want them to be. Then allow the feeling of gratitude to grow so that it reaches beyond any reason and just seems to generate joy in your experience of being grateful. Swim in it and record your responses.

- Now pick anything absolutely at random in your environment without any relation whatsoever to any sense of it having any reason or purpose in your life except the fact of its present "here and now-ness" (crumbs on the kitchen table, a fly buzzing in the air, a patch of green lawn out of a window, the angle of branches in a tree, the smell of the ground after a summer rain, the silent presence of your cat, the distant singing of your neighbor, the feel of a warming breeze, the rustle of leaves, the texture of your clothes, the smoothness of a stone, the taste of your own saliva, etc. etc.). Let your sense of gratitude flow out of you as free of thought and observation as you are inclined in the moment to allow it to flow. Thoughts, reasons may come. Do not resist or involve yourself with them, but just let them wash over you. Be more and more allowing of the pure sense of gratitude for the mere existence of whatever it is you are observing/experiencing. See the degree to which you can begin to rejoice in the simple reality of its being a springboard to your own deepening sense of gratitude and joy in just Being, just existing and savoring the wonder of it here and now! When you can, record your experiences.

- Start a *"gratitude journal."* Make note every day of your experiences with feeling gratitude and enjoy reviewing how it evolves and expands to include more and more of what you experience.

AWE

Absolutely anything at all can occasion your joy and your awe. Joy is the sense of intense delight with your experience of yourself and of the world in the infinitely varied ways in which you interpret the reality of any given moment. It is specific to some context, intra- and/or interpersonal or inter relational in some manner (could be other people or things, a fly on the wall!). Awe is joy that often springs out of a perception of some facet of reality as seen in a manner or relationship that you had not noticed before. (See the section on *God and Spirituality* and *Reflections* ahead for examples) A startling clarity of understanding is achieved that suddenly becomes more and more decontextualized not only encompassing the specific instance that you have taken as the point of evoking the experience, but also expanding suddenly to include a dimension of the totality of all things. Boundaries simply drop away and there is an instantaneous coming together of every aspect of your self-awareness into a singularity of almost blinding, light filled understanding. You are catapulted beyond the normal understanding of intensity to a place of utter calm and peacefulness and in the instant you are in that state, there is a sense of knowing absolutely everything that there is to know, above all, the truth about your happiness. You experience yourself as totally without desire or inclinations of any kind whatsoever.

Indeed if you become aware of your body in that state, you will find that every corner of your physical being is totally engaged in the experience. Let your awareness range from your hair to your toes, from your skin deep into the joints of your bones, from your tongue, the nipples of your breasts, into your genital region. All is one, all is completely and utterly satisfied to be one with you and your experience. There is not a single discordant mode of being in all your self-awareness. Awe is the closest description of what I call the basic ground state of being absolutely without any desire, want or inclination. It is just happiness, joy, elation folded into one singular truth of happiness in being. From this point of total freedom come the creative forays into the world as we know it. Out of that moment of ultimate rest and ultimate motion, we make ourselves up with whatever wants and desires we may choose to have. When we have the experience of awe, we instantly know the truth about our wanting and our total freedom from it at one and the same moment of clarity. Often a spontaneous reordering of our priorities takes place in response to this, a reordering that is comfortable and free of dread.

From this vantage point, you can become aware of how all-encompassing your freedom to create yourself is. Literally anything that is not you is simply the raw material of the grand playground that is the world. Select anything at all and become enthusiastic about it, a sonata of Beethoven or a speck of dust on your dining room table, made visible by the slanting rays of an early morning sun streaming through your kitchen window. You are the greatest living actor in the play of your life. Know that while the contextual props and circumstances of the physical universe are subject to the laws of uncertainty and the incompleteness theorem[*] the attitude toward whatever is, is entirely scripted by you. Throw yourself into your own story with all the zest and gusto your present sense of happiness will allow. You are always at the center of the universe, an unmoving singular point of consciousness watching the march of reality as it parades by you in never ending motions. All is in motion except you, even your body and its mind boggling levels of complexities are in constant fluctuation. You sit at that magisterial point of nowhere while your body, your mind or the circumstances of the physical world take you to whatever "somewheres" you may manage to discover. Remember the aperture for the present is about one half second long. Everything else outside that tiny moment of nowness is dream-like, gone, no longer existent. It is in moments of awe that the full extent of the *now* comes bursting forth with blinding potentials for joy. Opening up to awe is the exact opposite of closing down with dread. The perspective of dread would have you believe that all ends in a whimper of deadened stationarity, frozen in postures of endless regret and seething impotence. But the perspective of awe is refulgent with the ever expanding light of your freedom to be your happiness *now*.

QUESTIONS

- Do you fear your happiness? Do you fear what it could be like to surrender any Dread and be totally with whatever might be a part of your awareness now?
- Can you recall any experiences of awe? Make a list and enjoy your memories.

EXPER/CISES

---

[*] A nifty mathematical formula by the famous mathematician Goedel that describes how, at least in one dimension of it, nobody's control strategies can succeed in confining the universe into anyone's theoretical, ideological straitjacket.

- Your happiness can be seen as the medium on which you float. Watching ducks move leisurely across the surface of a bay with the water seen as shimmering effervescently underneath them is an image that is attractive to me. The idea is that it is an ever-present reality for you, the loving hum that hovers about you and instantly is there if you but listen. While your happiness can be heard and felt above the loudest din imaginable, still for many if not most, it is helpful on a regular basis to find a quiet place or simply to quiet your mind in the place you are in. Just give yourself over to being in touch with that basic rhythm, sound, feeling, energy, sense of utter equanimity that resides within your most intimate experience of yourself. Some may call this meditation, and that is fine. But what we are creating is not a preferred state of experience, but merely a tool to help realize the truth of our happiness more deeply. The word "enjoy" fits most aptly here, because what it means is to take the experience of joy that we have and to amplify and build upon it so that we have more and more joy. Therefore these states of self-observation are facilitative and not ends in themselves. The section on *Reflections* will be the most helpful in inspiring breakthroughs to awe in your life.

GOD AND SPIRITUALITY[1]

It should be made clear that the Option Method and your **Joywork** places no requirement for you to have some specific belief about a God or no God. No, of course you are quite free to come to your own sense of

---

[1] Some material in this Chapter appeared in an article I authored for *the Psycho-spiritual-transformation Journal.* The web address is http://psychospiritualresearchinstitute.com/god_and_spirituality.htm.

what anything like this could mean to you. So you are certainly free to take what follows, literally, metaphorically or to find no relevance in it for you at all. Your happiness does not depend on your allegiance to any vision of the divine or lack of it. At the same time, it is both fun and licit to speculate about what the notion of God could mean since it has been with us from the dawn of human self-reflection, as far as we can tell.

Humans have turned to God as the ultimate resource for meaning in their lives. Meaning is simply another word for happiness. Life has meaning to the degree that it offers hope of happiness. Now, okay, okay. What does "meaning" mean? First we are talking about it exclusively from the point of view of happiness. If you look at the world in terms of "B" then meaning comes exclusively from controlling the world. People and institutions are the most likely source of meaning in that understanding. You are with me, okay? So, when you say "something has meaning for me or gives my life meaning," aren't you saying that you are acknowledging that whatever *"It"* is that supposedly gives the meaning, **you** are the one giving yourself permission to feel good feelings about it? Still in doubt? Then let me ask you: can something give meaning to your life **against your will?** Sounds ridiculous, right? So of course not. What meaning is, is always the same—a permission from *you* to feel some kind of good or positive feeling about yourself or the world based on *your* understanding gained through the comprehension of whatever it is that *you* define as the something that "gives meaning to my life!" So where does the meaning come from really? Why from *you*, of course. You see when you switch from the logic of "B" to an understanding of the world from the "C" perspective, then the truth of what is going on becomes clear. It is tantamount to saying that "I give meaning to the things that give me meaning!" Yes and in mathematics 1+0=1! Adding more zeros will not change the outcome. Do you see? If the buck stops with you in terms of whether something means anything or not, then *you are the meaning giver.*

The world may be filled with a wonder of things that "catch your eye," so to speak and to which you give meaning. But nothing in the world can have meaning for you without your decision that it does. Therefore, life has meaning because you, the meaning giver give it meaning by *affirming* (from its root meaning to make firm or real) the truth about your happiness through each moment that you live it!

Now God has been used to foist a good deal of gray notions about unhappiness upon humans as well. God has been the handmaiden of cultures in attempting to constrain and intimidate people into being the way the culture wanted its citizens to be. And by culture I mean the evolving will of the generations of members of a society as evidenced in its traditions, customs, covenants and laws. We are not interested in any such usage of the notion of God.

What is the purpose of God then? Well if we edit out the uses of God as punisher, destroyer and enforcer for the unhappy religious visions of humans, then the true shape of the divine begins to emerge for what it really is. What we turn to God for, what we want from the divine, what the prayers and pleas of humans over the ages have amounted to has been a call for permission to be happy. When God becomes merely a figurehead for the minions who would enforce the edicts of culture, then the affection of humans for God wanes. In our own age, despite religious fundamentalism and the events of 9/11, many people find little use for a God so employed and so are quite alienated from any such concept. However, when God becomes the God of Joy and Awe, then the notion of God in our lives begins to hold the promise of a totally different reality.

What I would propose in accordance with what I learned through the Method, is that for God to have any meaning whatsoever, God must be our happiness. This is not hard to figure. If we think of God as the ultimate meaning giver, then what is it we want from God? That's right. Our happiness. And if we take it from the point of view of ourselves as the meaning givers to our lives and all in the world, what is the meaning we wish our lives to have? Why, you guessed it. Happiness, of course. Without happiness, would anything else in existence have any meaning for you? All the money in the world and no happiness? All the power in the world and no happiness? I know, I know, from the perspective of the logic of "B" you may still believe that those things in the world—wealth, power, sex, admiration, etc.—are the things that have the power to render meaning, to *make* you happy.

Hopefully at this juncture in your Joywork a dent has been made in those assumptions. For, no matter what you try to replace your happiness with, you end up wanting what? Why you guessed right again. Your happiness, of course. And that is precisely what God is: our happiness. An Old Testament psalm calls God the one "who gives joy." The divine in us is lived and experienced as our happiness, our joy, our elation, our felicity, our peace, our gratitude and awe. As my teacher opened my eyes to see, God is the experience of our happiness lived in us from moment to moment. What humans have always wanted God to be, that is the source of endless joy, lo and behold, that is what God is! The divine lives in us through our experience of our freedom and happiness. This is the substance, the life, the breath of God being actualized in the moment to moment realization of our joy. Joy, happiness is the *pneuma,* the life breath of God. Your happiness is literally God's breath, the divine respiration, the compassionate metabolism of joy.

It is reasonable to assume, therefore, that our living our lives in the light of our freedom and happiness is fulfilling the will of the divine. We know that our love is a gift of spontaneity and freedom, unconditioned by any cause. So too, the Divine love is the same. What we offer in loving is the fullness of our wish for the happiness of the beloved. When we see those we love living and experiencing their joy, then their joy becomes our joy.

How could that be any less with God? Surely God's joy is our joy. As we live it, we not only have the fullness of all we could ever want, but we can revel in the knowledge that through our joy we are fulfilling the grandest design of the divine for us, in us.

That brings us to the notion around which this chapter is built: God and Spirituality. We have defined God as happiness, the one who gives joy. The primary quality of the divine is freedom because it is out of that understanding of the divine that we can legitimately describe creation as an act of love. Without freedom, we have the spectacle of some kind of unmoved mover who accidentally belched in the void and hasn't a clue that in doing so it set in motion the evolution of the universe[s] as we know it. We value what we call love precisely because it is an outcome of freedom that thrives best and is fully nurtured by our happiness. So the *spiritual* we can take in general terms to be the more intimate experience of the self; that which touches upon, relates to, or manifests in a more singular way the deeper characteristics of meaning of a person. The spiritual is the tabernacle of our deepest values. Our experience of our freedom and happiness constitute both the fundamental dynamics of the self and the creative, generative matrix out of which comes the living moment to moment performance of the truth of ourselves. So the ongoing experience of being spiritual is a continuing sense of consonance with that generative matrix within ourselves.

I would also posit that the living performance of our spirituality in each moment can be captured by a number of states of experience: **Hope, Compassion, Gratitude, Presence, Spontaneous Action** and **Joy**. There are other additional characteristics but for the purposes of this writing I wish to focus on these six because collectively and synergistically they together form what I call the **Attitude**; that is an ongoing stance and momentum that inclines us in the direction of more consistently affirming our happiness and joy in each moment. The happiness loop illustrated here gives an outline of what is to follow.

THE HAPPINESS LOOP: All unhappiness derives from the fundamental belief that you have to be unhappy; this is multiplied in all the many ways unhappiness takes its forms. So too happiness is rooted in the knowing Affirmation of the truth about happiness, cultivated in the moment to moment realization of the Attitude: I am my happiness and there is nothing I could know or experience that can deprive me of this.

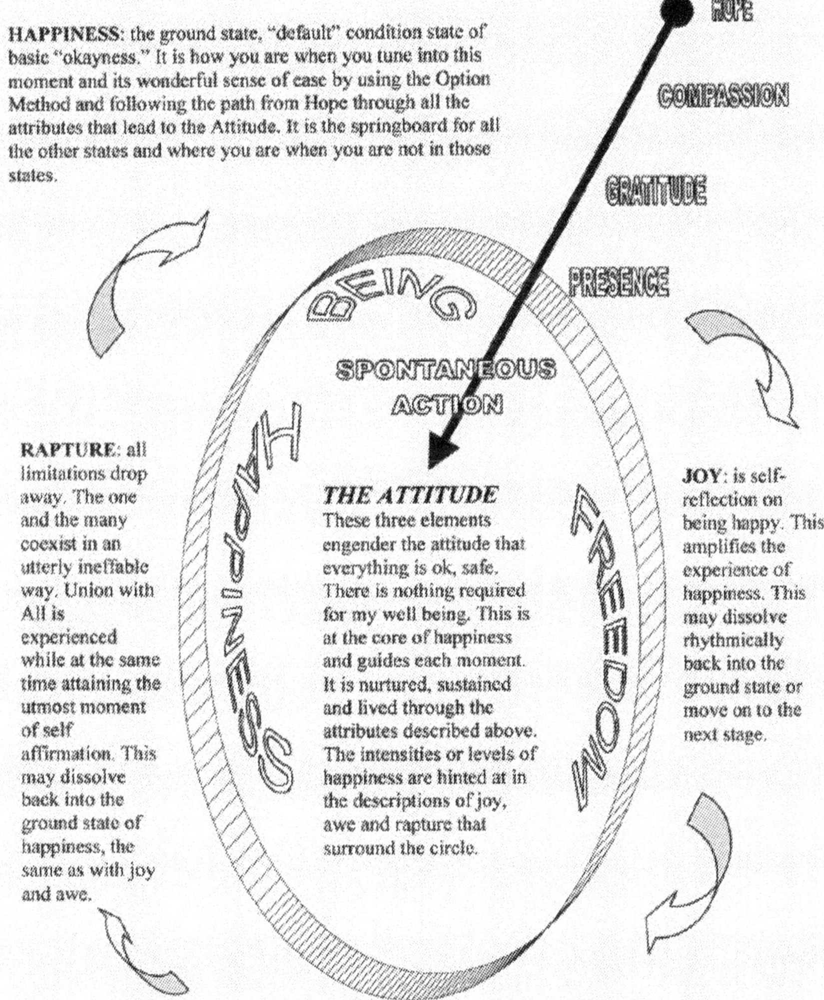

HAPPINESS: the ground state, "default" condition state of basic "okayness." It is how you are when you tune into this moment and its wonderful sense of ease by using the Option Method and following the path from Hope through all the attributes that lead to the Attitude. It is the springboard for all the other states and where you are when you are not in those states.

RAPTURE: all limitations drop away. The one and the many coexist in an utterly ineffable way. Union with All is experienced while at the same time attaining the utmost moment of self affirmation. This may dissolve back into the ground state of happiness, the same as with joy and awe.

THE ATTITUDE
These three elements engender the attitude that everything is ok, safe. There is nothing required for my well being. This is at the core of happiness and guides each moment. It is nurtured, sustained and lived through the attributes described above. The intensities or levels of happiness are hinted at in the descriptions of joy, awe and rapture that surround the circle.

JOY: is self-reflection on being happy. This amplifies the experience of happiness. This may dissolve rhythmically back into the ground state or move on to the next stage.

AWE: is the further reflection that builds on Joy. It catches some aspect of reality in its pristine newness. Like a child seeing a cat for the first time. This is the "eyes of a child" experience of uniqueness. As with joy, it may revert to the ground state of happiness or move on to Rapture.

Hope: is the door that unlocks the heart to the truth of happiness. While many of course already possess hope because they experience happiness in however a contained way that might apply, still others who live in more desperate existential moments find hope the glimpse of the promised land they thought an impossible dream. Just as being afraid of unhappiness, or of becoming unhappy is already being unhappy, so too, being hopeful of happiness, however tiny an opening in that direction there may be, is already being happy! While hope is the primary movement toward happiness, compassion is often its secret companion that helps to soften the defensiveness of cynicism, despair and the dark assumptions of so many years with the warmth of even an instant's kind regard toward oneself.

Compassion: In the employment of the Option Method by people there is initially often a period when the person has had a wonderful experience of liberation by virtue of understanding that some aspect of their unhappiness is not necessary and they have permission to feel good and do in fact feel those good feelings. Such moments though are usually followed by a return to the well worn patterns of unhappiness. The person then may typically feel as if they are a failure because they have not maintained their good feelings. They do not recognize that the judgment about themselves is what now stands in the way of successfully using the Method to continue to clear away beliefs in unhappiness. It is at that point that I introduce the concept of Compassion. What I hope is obvious is that by Compassion I do not in any way mean somehow feeling bad or unhappy because someone else is feeling bad or unhappy. What I mean by this is a sense of loving concern that takes the emotional form of tenderness towards ourselves for having done the best we know to do even when that means a failure to achieve goals or to be consonant with what we normally hold as values important to us. The judgment dissolves and with it the block to continuing to allow ourselves to open up to our happiness. Humor, especially when focused non judgmentally upon oneself can be a wonderful lubricant to loosen the encrusted bolts that bind us to prisons we make with our beliefs in unhappiness. Compassion guarantees, at a minimum, a cycle of remembrance and return to the affirmation of happiness.

Gratitude: What immediately floods in following Compassion is the powerful healing state of Gratitude; that sense of warmth and tenderness introduced by Compassion increases many fold as we realize that we were the ones who allowed ourselves to feel good even in the face of recent deficits in our hopes and dreams, even in the face of an entire life filled with such existential potholes on the paths we hoped would lead us to certain levels of attainment in our relations with others and with the world at large. Many times we feel this in our body as a gentle or intense wave of physical relief and growing emotional élan, like a sudden cooling breeze by the shore on a stifling day that sweeps across your body turning every pore into a receptacle for ease and elation. Gratitude is the divine fuel that feeds and sustains the Attitude.

Presence: As Gratitude becomes more a tradition and enduring place we come to inhabit with greater regularity, we enter into a state I call "Presence" which is the experience of a quiet ease and confidence in being with oneself and with others. Issues as problems having to do with any threat to our happiness do not exist; issues as having to do with the practical workings of the world around us are related to with as much intelligence as we can bring to bear without any compulsion or sense of necessity. Having had the privilege of having dogs and cats as companions for so many years gives me a wonderful model of Presence. Their states of restfulness are not merely neutral down times; anyone who has been with their pets over the years comes to treasure those times of the day when your companion is present to you. This is what Martin Buber describes at one point in his classic work *I And Thou*, in his own experience with a cat, a sense of canniness and unexpected recognition that invites and celebrates being with in the profound and wordless fashion of I and Thou.

Spontaneous Action: Out of the depths of the silent pond of Presence often emerges the unpredictable surge I call Spontaneous Action. So many times when we are strangled with our fears and anxieties, every decision can be an agony of doubt and distress about possible outcomes and undesirable effects. In the quiet comfort that Presence provides we can be in touch with our freedom in ways that are stifled by our normal belief systems. We can make decisions and act on them with a seamless ease and comfort that surprises and delights us. Letting go of the fearful observer that we often put in place to monitor all our behaviors is further a manifestation of the degree to which we have opened ourselves up to trust in who we are, how we are free to proceed with our life without dread. There are no claims to infallibility here, merely of a loving confidence that we cannot be bad for ourselves even when our actions in the world fall short of getting us what we want.

Presence can be a cradle for Spontaneous Action to birth many initiatives consonant with our values. Out of our happiness in loving, we could also know, should we choose to, the joy of the divine in feeding the hungry, in comforting the dying, in teaching those who hunger for knowledge; we could know the joy of the divine in loving the happiness that is resident in all humans, in all creation, even when those humans and that creation do not seem to comprehend or reflect that knowing. This is no imperative, just the abundance of playfulness that could be a miracle for ourselves and our fellow humans. No constraining orthodoxy or crushing models of "authenticity" are extant here. Rather what I call the Great Democracy of Being is reflected in the fluid dynamics of the **Attitude** alive in us. That means that everyone has always immediate and unmediated access to their happiness in each and every instant of their lives.

Here is a true wonder for us to contemplate if we are inclined to do so. And let me add, that part of the wonder of being present and living our happiness is that there is never anything that has to constrain whatever we could come to know. There is no such thing as "dangerous" knowledge, because there is nothing we could come to know that can compel us to be a way we do not want to be against our will. The happier we are, the clearer we are about the joy of knowing and the closer we move to the divine sense that knowing is being. ***To know our happiness is to be our*** *happiness.* So our openness to all that is, is without limit, since knowing is never a danger, but a potential door to joy, understood through the divine sense of knowing one's happiness. This is the only legitimate instance where knowing is being for all of us because it is the only absolutely unambiguous case where what we know, our happiness, is completely within our control. All other knowing is conditional knowing, pertaining to the phenomenal and not the noumenal core of being.

Joy: Finally we come to joy and in joy we close the loop begun with Compassion. Joy is the reflexive act of recognition that indeed we are happy. It is a particular form of attention to our success in affirming the truth of happiness in which we literally rejoice in the achievement of that state. This recognition then becomes a platform for the amplification of our good feelings. They reverberate like the waves of a tuning fork reinforcing one another and as it were strengthening the force of the vibration. It fuels the growth and maintenance of the Attitude and fosters its expansion into the still dim and unlit corners of our self experience. It can open the inner doors of our minds to the beatific vision of **Awe** that is the core of our sense of union with the divine, a union that maintains what Russian literary master and philosopher Dostoevsky calls the "mystery of the individual" while at the same time uniting us with all of creation in the realm that the mystic/physicist David Bohm terms the "implicate order."

And so Spirituality is the manifesting of the Attitude in all its dimensions. It is the fulfillment of our purpose in existing which is to be happy. All other roles in life are essentially our playing in the world. There is never any guarantee that any particular role will be granted to us or that acting in that role we will live up to the demands and standards of any particular cultural paradigm that might be extant at the time of our historical existence. Thus our true purpose can only be what we can actually fulfill and that is fulfilled every time we affirm our happiness in any given moment. For any instant is not in time, but rather time is in that instant, that space we call the present which is our experience of the eternal. Our relationship with God is nurtured then by our spiritual evolving of the

Attitude. It is following that deep innate prompting to manifest the trinity of the self: Being, Freedom, Happiness—all different facets of the same underlying reality. Moving in concert with that fundamental rhythm is a resonance with the divine. It is a plucking on the ontological strings whose melody is the creative symphony of evolving life. Listen to it in every breath and movement of your body and in every crack, crevice and living surface of nature and rejoice in the light of God's truth: ***you living your Joy now!***

QUESTIONS

- Do you know that God is your happiness; that the divine lives through your affirmation of your happiness? What God *feels* like is you being happy!
- Do you have any reservations about living the joy of the divine in you? What would hold you back from rejoicing in such a notion?

EXER/CISES

- 1. Use the notion that God is your happiness to explore increasing the intensity and quality of your love for others. 2. Be in touch with the wonder and awe of the rhythms of nature by going to some special place and feeling the joy of solitude while being in the full presence of all the manifestations of nature around you. Joy resonates in each blade of grass, in each bird's cry, in every swirl of the tides and movement of the wind, in all the starry brilliance of the night sky. 3. Open yourself up to all of this and feel the joy of loving even more those who in turn love their happiness.
- Take some time to contemplate the wonder of humor. Laughter is one of the more self-evident manifestations of living your joy. Give

 yourself over to more of it and expand the **"happy nut"** aspect of yourself. Without a fear of ever being "foolish" you may find that the **comedic in you is also the divine**, that all that is, is the harmonic echo of the laughter of God resonating in our hearts as we live our joy. Find the comic lovingly every day and record what you experience so you can enjoy it over and over again[*].

JOY FOREVER!

Well, if you have gotten this far, it must hopefully mean that you have found the journey of value. Of course, you may just be perusing this workbook and immediately came to this section because this is the payoff, isn't it. Joy forever! That is what you want, why you would be interested in the Option message and in entering upon your Joywork in the first place. Well if that is the case, then I would urge you to take the time to use the workbook in a more systematic sense so that this last section can have the meaning for you that I know it can hold once you have made the discoveries about your happiness that the earlier sections are designed to help elicit. But of course read on if that is your delight. To those who have made their way through this Joybuilding System , let me address in a summary sense the potential for you that is your birthright and hopefully has been more fully actualized by your use of the Method and all the accompanying materials.

There is no trick in speaking of "Joy Forever." Rather, what we have come to understand on all levels about the nature of our happiness serves to reinforce the notion that this is a realistic way of comprehending the truth of your happiness. After all, you live your existence one moment at a time, just as we have described it. You cannot do otherwise, even though

---

[*] My novel *The God-Speak* has some interesting discussions of a similar character.

through our minds and imaginations, we may contrive to believe we are "living" in the past, or somehow experiencing the future. The truth is that we are always living in the eternal present, experienced one frame at a time. And, as we earlier pointed out, nothing outside of that frame in any way has the power to compromise our decision about how we are going to experience it. When we affirm our joy in any given moment, it is our being in touch with the eternal present. It is the only equivalent of the word "forever" that there is. We get a sense of something as being ongoing when we repeat the experience over and over again. However, that sense is merely a convenient way of helping in our comprehension of the way the material world operates in space and time. Our window of truth is always just now, never any other time, but just now. So when we want our joy forever, our happiness forever, we sometimes mean, from the perspective of unhappiness, that we want to end our freedom to be whatever way it seems appropriate for us to be in a given moment, because we do not trust ourselves to affirm our happiness. This mistrust of ourselves and our freedom is what is at the heart of unhappiness and derives as well from a misunderstanding of time along the lines detailed in our discussions earlier. We are not against ourselves. Even in our most apparently entangled thrashing about in unhappiness, we are really only trying to ameliorate what we consider to be the inevitable nature of being human, i.e., being unhappy.

By now as you have joyworked your way through the many explanations, questions and suggested experiential exercises, it has hopefully come more fully to your awareness that what you really want is your happiness and that this want can be exercised only now in this very moment. Yes, what you hopefully have learned at this juncture is that your wanting your happiness, your love for your joy, your freedom from any sense that there is anything wrong with either happiness or unhappiness or with any way you might have been or might be: all of that can lovingly conspire to reassure you that you *are* your happiness and it is only a matter of affirming that *now!* Instead of dreading the unfolding of each moment, you can begin to look forward to each and every one, no matter what the context or circumstances, because nothing can come between you and your happiness, except your decision not to affirm it. And that decision cannot veto or encumber any moment but the actual one in which it is made. Instantly, a new vista opens up for you to affirm otherwise.

In other words, now is always an open reality, beckoning and ready to be the vessel for the expression of your joy. You have but to fill it up with the knowledge of your being happy and it will bubble in the clarifying light of that instant, effervescent and lucent with the elixir of elation. That is how each moment greets you. If you forget that at any time, then like a light shining out of the darkness to a traveler returning home, there is always the welcome embrace of remembering your joy in the next moment. There is always the nonjudgmental truth of your happiness standing on the threshold of the temple of the next moment ready to initiate the festival of your joy like loving parents who cannot wait to offer their child the fruits and warmth of their/ your eternal home in the now, the everlasting now, the kingdom of yourself, the wellspring of your freedom to love, this time, this unbridled ocean of surging awe, your experience of living your JOY FOREVER!

QUESTIONS

- Do you really want the case you make for your unhappiness to carry the day? Do you want to "win" your pleas that all reasonable people just experience unhappiness, that it is organic, natural, humanizing; that it adds fullness, depth and dimension to human experience; that not to feel it would actually be harmful and even cause you physical harm because your "denial" would cause unconscious tensions that would elaborate themselves malignantly in your physiology, etc.? What remarkable advocates we are for our unhappiness, untiring prosecutors of ourselves as defendants charged with wanton disregard of the cultural laws against the felonies of joy and elation.

To hear ourselves filled with indignation over how terrible it would be to be happy in such and such a case is to be reminded of the trials of witches and political dissidents. It is to know just how ideologically constrained we are by what we think we know and embrace. What an empty victory to "defeat" your happiness and be crowned as an "orthodox" member of culture's "victorious" legions all marching in lockstep to anthems of righteousness and moral certainty. Fortunately, because your happiness is part of the very fabric of who your are, you cannot really "defeat" it. You can only live as if it did not exist for you. But it does and it will always be patiently waiting in the spirit of the last paragraph of this section's description.

- Well my friend, you have gone through this workbook at least once to be at this point. That is a good deal of Joywork completed. While you may have other aspects of yourself you have identified as wanting to be different, now is the time for your JOY. Are you ready to give yourself over to the loving, compassionate embrace of your own happiness? Through your freedom can you simply "freefall" into the awesomeness of the uncensored, unlimited, uninhibited, unconditional truth of your happiness? DO IT! Feel the winds of elation flowing over you as you fall, or better yet as you rise, since direction is meaningless. There is just you, the loving you, the playful you, the endlessly knowing you, the divine you, moving through space and time and yet motionless and connected to all in the center of yourself, in the center of being. Can you be in touch with the immense gratitude that you feel to yourself for allowing yourself to affirm your happiness, for giving yourself the immeasurable gift of your joy without end NOW, and for all the nows without end? ENJOY AND BE YOUR HAPPINESS NOW! CONGRATULATIONS!

CHAPTER SEVEN

REFLECTIONS/IMAGES

REFLECTIONS

Certainly it was the human being that was elected to bring
Values to the world…and his place of good is the knowledge
Of all things, joy at all times, freedom from anxiety and
Freedom from fear of the enemy.
Orunmila, the god of divination in the African tradition.

The purpose of this section is to give you some idea of how to establish a tradition of observation and reflection that supports the Attitude and the ongoing experience of your happiness. All of these reflections would most helpfully be understood as patterns rather than absolute formulas to be followed. Many of the images I use will be those of the sea and the shore. Anyone could just as usefully substitute any context/image they wish or find congenial. The idea is to help to open you up to the potentials for being in touch with the joy inherent in everything around you. As you train your eyes and all your senses to become sensitive to these possibilities, you will be richly rewarded by what you will discover. They will be your discoveries, meaningful to you in very specific ways. So do write them down in as much detail as you can muster.

Note please that all of the following reflections, with the possible exception of my reflections on the death of my dog, Nicki, are about small events in my life. Nothing earth shattering by most standards is described. That is important. Of course there are "larger" issues/events in everyone's life and you can certainly reflect and record your experiences as it seems appropriate for you to do so. But most of life is a series of small pearls of occurrences strung together from birth to death. My goal was to illustrate how these small pearls of observations can spark deep and intense instants of joy and satisfaction. They can support your desire to be happier because you sharpen your senses and bring the nurturing balm of gratitude to all levels of your sensory array.

Start with a perception/experience and just give yourself a couple of words to fix the important aspects of that experience. When you have time later, then you can begin to elaborate on it. It may be that something you come upon now has associative links to things in your memory of times past. That's just fine. What is important is simply to do it, not to hold back because your approach and way of writing is not like mine or does not conform to some other standard you may have in your head. As Aunt Rose used to say, if you don't wash the tomatoes, you don't get the sauce. So come on!

They will be always waiting for you in this Joybook, this fruit of your Joywork, ready to rekindle the beauty of the moment you captured and to renew your contact with the wellsprings of your happiness. After each of my reflections, please write in one of your own in your notebook. These are only meant to prime the pump of your own elation. My words and manner of describing things are simply my own. They have no special value except hopefully to expose the joy I felt and feel in the actual moment of the experience and every time I read them again. There is no end to this book. Your self creation can be chronicled on these pages and all the ones you add without limit. I invite you to taste the sweetness of creation and all the gifts it brings. ***May the bliss of your knowing the truth about happiness be always with you!***

IMAGES:

PEOPLE

- I recently moved and in the course of digging out years of accumulated "life stuff" I came across an old pot. At first the sight of this begrimed and battered object inclined me to toss it immediately upon the nearby junkpile ready to be wrapped as a "gift" for the garbage pickup. But then something inside me made me pause and I got a sudden glint of recognition. This was none other than one of Aunt Rose's garlic browning pots. God only knows how old it actually was with its rounded belly, narrowing down to a flat bottom. On the sides were curved metal handles with black wooden spools for gripping the pot. I brought it close and looked at the black and brown marks on the outside and some places on the inside. Irreducible residues of a thousand and one infusions of garlic, oil followed by spices, pork, bracciole, meatballs, sausage, tomato paste, fresh tomatoes, or other staples of Southern Italian cooking. Like an Italian version of Proust's "madelaine and cup of tea," I instantly had a remembrance of the fragrance that filled the kitchen in her home on so many occasions.

  It was the signature piece of her existence. She moved around from stove to counter, shifting pots on the burners, deftly opening oven doors, elegantly retrieving utensils, spices, ingredients from drawers, cabinets and refrigerator with the élan and directorial authority of a Bernstein conducting Beethoven's ninth. Her ever increasing enormous girth seemed so negligible as she literally glided effortlessly across a tiled floor doing amazing pirouettes and Burmese like motions with her upper body, shoulders, arms and hands. How exactly was this *Excalibur* of culinary remembrance passed on to me? Ah yes, at one point, she gave it to my mother who in turn passed it along to me and my family. We never really used it. Somehow, you could not scrub off the patina of all that cooked-in garlic, tomato and spice. It could not be made to shine and sparkle like a new pot with no history, and I guess at one point we did not value the history that Aunt Rose represented. So it was consigned to the exile of a dark cellar awaiting the day of resurrection and reinstatement. Well it never quite got to that stage, I must confess, but what it represented—a love of life and food— certainly had already been brought to vivid life. So, fingering the pot with its bumps, grit and gnarled surfaces was like reliving those moments, with their bizarre mixture of the ancient and the new. Like the time she gave us some live chickens to take home. So we all piled into my father's old '38 ford, my father, mother, brother, grandmother, chickens and me and we got stuck in a grand traffic jam returning from New Jersey (where Aunt Rose had her abode) to New York in August, in the middle of the Holland tunnel in the days when cars had no air conditioning. Madonna, what a stew of sounds, smells, exotic expressions and sweat that was.

Now as I remember I am filled with gratitude for the appreciation of food and life that that pot represented. Its aromas were like caresses, spreading the sweetness of the message that life is always now in the midst of all the tumult and untidiness, sweat and voices raised above the din. So grab a little garlic, extra virgin olive oil, a few sprigs of basil, parsley and mint and give a toss just long enough to tan, not ever to burn and proceed as your spirit takes you. Your life will taste as sweet as you allow your joy to make it!

• I was deep into the middle of a revision of this very book one afternoon when the phone rang. A pleasant but somewhat muffled voice innocently inquired as to whether this was Options For Living. I answered affirmatively and the voice further inquired as what it was that was done there. Now, understand, I get phone calls with the same kind of inquiry with some varying regularity, and to the degree that I can I try to accommodate the people calling. So I went into a short spiel about what I was about. The voice interrupted me and asked if I would make a determination as to whether her problem fit the profile of what I did. I attempted to interject that whatever her problem, I was probably not going to be available for a few months, but the voice spoke politely but insistently over mine, informing me that she was a female who really wanted to be a male and was seriously thinking of having an operation to accomplish this, and by, the by, did we do anything like that at Options For Living.

Well, gentle reader I spent many years dealing with all kinds of problems and so nothing really surprises me. This was a bit exotic, but by far not off the scale of what humans are concerned about. So, I politely answered no, and attempted to move the conversation toward closure, but the voice kept asking about my availability and capability to accommodate some of her small eccentricities. She worked very odd hours, so could I see her close to midnight and she always traveled with her three dogs because she would never leave them home, so would that be a problem? Well, there was a pause as I considered the kindest way to terminate our talk, when the voice asked also did I mind if she brought her own coffee pot, since it really comforted her to make her own coffee in a special way. Silence. I began to seriously respond to the voice, when all of a sudden it let out a great howl of laughter that continued for a moment or two. The voice suddenly changed its timbre and the familiar sound of my oldest step-daughter came through the receiver, broken up with tears of hilarity. "It's me, Frankie doodle," she said. Boy, had I *been had.* We both broke up for a moment or two. Yes, I had been had, *lovingly had,* caringly fooled, by one who loved to play practical jokes all of her life. While our conversation turned to more conventional matters of family and career, I felt such gratitude for having in my life those who care about me enough to contrive ways to "get me." Being loved is always a wonder, always a gateway into awe.

- In early summer, my wife and I had the pleasure of taking two of our grandchildren for a trip of several days to Watkin's Glen, a gorge some few miles long, and 100 or more feet deep, created by a small river (that flows into Lake Cayuga) over many thousands of years after the last ice age. The two girls, Brittany and Chelsea, both between six and seven, sat in the back and engaged us for many hours in different games and puzzles, one of which was designed in such a way that the goal was to get you to say "What." When you said "What," you then had the task of "getting rid of it," in five minutes, by tricking someone else into saying "What." Now you would think that, once you knew the object of the game, you would be immune to being fooled into saying "What," especially since we were adults and of course so much more clever that mere six year olds.

  Well, as we rolled down the highway, innocent, sweet little voices would plaintively call out: "Grandpa, Grandma," to which either of us would answer: "Yes," or "Hmmm," or anything but the *dreaded* word, "What." How easy it was to defeat their deliriously obvious attempts to fool sophisticated adults like us! Time passed in silent self-satisfaction. Then came a blood curdling scream, followed by tears of such intensity, that I pulled the car off the road and we both turned and yelled in unison: "WHAAAT." Silence, tears are drying on a face that is smiling triumphantly as the demure, but confident little voice proclaims in sugary sing song tones: "Made you say it. Now you have five minutes to get rid of it!" Peals of laughter come from both the conspirators in the back seat. What a performance.

Crestfallen, we continued, filled with a renewed sense of respect for the inventiveness of six year olds and even more so filled with the wonder of how easy it is for them to just "make themselves up," with whatever intensities and shows of sincerity a situation might call for. Yes, yes, I know, there are things that they "really" will be miserable about at that age, but they are still in touch with the great latitude they have to use their emotions to play and gain advantage in the world without actually "suffering" the pangs of unhappiness, but merely, playing at it like an actor using the "Method." Indeed, during silent times in the journey, one or the other of them would literally "rehearse" scenes where strong emotions might be needed, trying various pitches of shouts and tones of being "hurt" and "outraged" at some imagined slight or downturn of fortune. How telling a lesson for us in self-creation. How wonderful a reminder that our feelings are a sort of "script" we have created to accommodate our beliefs. How liberating to return to that age of emotional invention in spirit and turn our being to the pleasures of building our joy with one another.

- Not long ago while we were out to dinner in a favorite Greek restaurant nearby, we sat outside on the patio portion, enjoying an early summer evening with what our friend Nick, the owner, prepared for us: wonderful haloumi cheese with local tomatoes, toasted on pita bread, a tangy, lemony spread of chick pea paste or hoummous, outstanding ripe black olives, followed by some superlative grilled fish with crunchily cooked vegies, done *al dente* the way we like them. At a table nearby sat a middle aged couple with a young daughter. They were speaking in Russian, a language I speak and understand from my days as a professor specializing in Russian literature and philosophy at New York University. Meeting and chatting with them was a pleasure, but the sound of that language and the trinity of father, mother, daughter, brought me back to another experience and it is that I now speak of.

Many years ago when I had just begun living in an apartment in New York, I returned one evening to find an elderly couple, a man and his wife, doing their chores as janitors of the building. I had not run into them before and as I approached them, I heard them speaking in Russian with one another. They had both been brought up in the Baltic area when it was part of Czarist Russia and so spoke Russian quite often, though they spoke several other languages as well. They turned in surprise as I greeted them in that language and an immediate friendship sprang up between us. I learned that they were actually quite a sophisticated couple, originally from Latvia in Eastern Europe, with a daughter, no longer living with them, who was a fairly successful opera singer. And it was true, often when I chanced to pass their small ground floor apartment, I would hear the recorded voice of their daughter, or some other wonderful classical pieces.

Now I was curious about them and over time learned that the husband had been a very important man in the Latvian government when Latvia enjoyed a short existence between World War I and II. With the fall of Latvia to the advancing Soviet army, he fled with his wife and young daughter, eventually coming to the United States. Whatever his talents in his native country, he did not have the language skills or training to find a comparable position in this country, so he did whatever fell to him to do, aided and supported by his wife, and they eventually ended up in the janitorial position when I met them.

At the time I was astounded by the fact that a man, a couple, that had achieved such prominence and material success in one cultural context, should be so resilient as to come to a foreign country and, unable to maintain their social standing, take menial labor and be so comfortable with what most people would describe as a major reversal of fortune. Certainly, they weren't able to control the way the world and the events of history displaced them like a horse's tale flicking a fly off its back. Yet never did I sense any rancor, disappointment or sour grapes in their attitude toward the world or their work. The floors were swept, mopped and kept sparkling with a synergy of labor that they both shared in loving routines.

Finally one day when I felt comfortable enough to do so, I broached the subject with them. How could it be that they were so happy when events had treated them so unkindly? Now this was some years before I came upon the perspective that I espouse in this book, so I was completely puzzled by their equanimity in dealing with this. The husband turned to me with a gentle smile and said: "When we were in our homeland, we did the very best we could in the work that we were fortunate enough to be able to do, and now, here, we do the same. We are the very best janitors that we know how to be. It is our pleasure to be so." The wife nodded here in smiling agreement. Then they left to continue their work, pushing their cart filled with mops and cleaning materials to another part of the apartment. I stood there not comprehending what I had heard, indeed not believing it. Years passed, and then I came to know the same truth. What a gift I had been given by their example so long ago in the past. What great fortune to have been able to unwrap that gift and make it my own by coming to know my joy.

- It is summer on the East End of Long Island, a time when this gorgeous landscape of ocean beaches, sound shores, bays, coves, rivers, lakes, ponds, open fields filled with corn, broccoli, vegies and, recently vineyards comes sparklingly alive with a huge influx of refugees of metropolitan New York and all over the world. Roads and stores that are relatively quiet and empty in the other seasons are now bustling with people going to the beaches or to whatever form of entertainment their hungry hearts may contrive to cook up. I am driving on old Montauk highway into Quogue to pick up some special cheese for baking pizza on the out door grill, an art which I have perfected to the point that would make the gods jealous. Aunt Rose would warn me soundly about the *malocchio* for rejoicing in my accomplishment! As I drive along in moderately heavy traffic listening to some jazz, a car behind me, a pickup truck with a very attractive young couple begins to beep the horn vociferously at me.

At first, I ignore them, assuming, incorrectly as you will see, that they are just a couple of "summer people" trying to move me along more quickly so they can get wherever it is they seem impatient, as I assume, to be getting to. Well, the beeping continues. I look in my rear view mirror and observe that the look on the faces of the two blonde and tanned young faces is not one of impatience, but of genuine hilarity and mirth. They are waving and pointing furiously at my car. Well, okay, hey maybe my tire is going flat or who knows, but let me pull over and see what it might be. I do so carefully. They pull over ahead of me and the young woman jumps out of the car to meet me as I emerge from my own vehicle. I know immediately from her face that the intent is warm and friendly; it shows in the brightness of her eyes and the absolute splendor of her smile. When she reaches me, I ask whether indeed they had noticed something wrong with my car, but she interrupts me in with her smile, gently takes my arm and turns me around to face the read end of the car. There, on the trunk sitting like farm dogs in the back of an open pickup are my wife's shoes, purse and a package of unshucked corn. I turn back to my benefactress who giggles, then laughs openly, knowingly, graciously. I mumble something incomprehensible as an explanation for their being there and then, my heart overflowing with gratitude, return her smile and thank her profusely, even as I also wave and nod to her young male companion in the truck ahead, who is also still waving and laughing.

What a moment! These two young people see the car ahead of them with the shoes, purse and corn perched on the trunk (remaining there with Lord knows whatever gravity defying steadfastness in the face of my having driven about four miles at that point) and divine in a flash somehow what has happened: absent minded middle-aged man drives away without realizing that home-returning middle-aged wife had dropped the items onto the trunk as she is wont to do when rushing in from work and tearing off to the nearby beach for an afternoon swim. Perhaps they were lovers on the way to a more permanent relationship and were humorously touched by what they instantly (as I surmise it to be anyway) understood was a moment in the domestic life of another couple that had advanced so far down the road that the display of absentmindedness was touching to them. Their joy in rendering a kindness to me was real and as they drove off, I sat for a moment or two as the traffic wound its way along side of me to a thousand destination points unknown. A thrill of elation and gratitude ran through my body over their simple act of caring. Truly there is rapture in the silliness of things unnoticed or even left undone. Whoever they were, they were open to their joy and available to their impulse to be helpful. By my being receptive, the moment of meeting and recognition, though only seconds in length, became an occasion for the exchange of mutual mirth, bountiful playfulness and the affirmation of our willingness to seize the moment and live it in our joy.

• A fair number of years ago when I was working as a psychotherapist in New York City, and before I had in any way formally adopted my present point of view, I chanced to briefly have a client who was made paranoid schizophrenic by the use of an anti-parkinsonian drug that was known to sometimes have that side effect. He had Parkinson's disease, a gradually debilitating neuromuscular disorder, for some years; beyond that fact about his disability, he was also a renowned scholar in his field and a man of great humor when his paranoid delusions were not so active and distracting. He professed a great deal of pain over what these delusional fantasies instructed him to do. You see he described a fearsome, dark, apocalyptic council of twelve that sat in his brain and sternly instructed him to commit all kinds of horrible acts, none of which he ever carried out. He was merely tortured by the constant chorus of these internal doomsayers and their never-ending drumbeat to either, blow up his office at the University where he taught, kill the Dean (an imperative those of us who have taught in higher education can sometimes well understand) or perform other dastardly deeds that went against all his considerable values as a kind and gentle scholar.

Now, not being armed with what I know today, but yet close to some of the notions that I now rejoice in, I decided to try enlist some of his wonderful character traits on his own behalf. So I asked him one day, "Stewart, have you ever tried telling those guys inside a joke?" He froze in his chair and looked at me with total disbelief, then replied: "Oh no Frank, you don't seem to understand, these guys don't know from humor. No, no with them it's only the same old song: "Stewart when are you going to kill the Dean. Stewart, have you pushed the secretary down the stairs as we instructed you to. Stewart, have you poisoned your wife's coffee as you were ordered, ' and on and on." He shook his head sadly, "No, no Frank, these guys don't even take time out to go to the bathroom, I mean, they are deadly serious."

"Well," I replied, "I can appreciate that, but look Stewart, what have you got to lose, hmmm? Go ahead and hit them with the one you told me last week, you know the one about the Rabbi and the donkey?" Stewart's face lightened up a bit with the recollection, but darkened at the prospect of sharing it with "the twelve." However, after some more cajoling he finally reconsidered and "went inside" as he called it to encounter the committee. His eyes turned up in his head as he made contact with them and it took what seemed like several minutes before he "returned" and focused back on me. There was a pause, and then a smile lit up his face. "Frank," he began, "At first when I started they began to scream and carry on something terrible, threatening me with the worst tortures and deeds imaginable. But I kept on and since I love the joke I really got into it. When I was done and delivered the punch line, there was silence. I thought 'Oh my gosh, they are going to be so pissed now.' But, you know the one on the very end with the tattoos, well, I could see him struggling to maintain his composure, but sure enough, he broke out into a few giggles, much to the disapproval of the rest of the committee, but nonetheless, the son of a bitch laughed!"

For Stewart, that was a moment of joy. While it took some creative doing to get the rest of the committee to relent in their ravings, Stewart now took hope in his ability to deliver his humor to himself and to bring some mirth into his delusional world. He had done what the famous mathematician John Nash had done in the face of his demanding delusions and hallucinations and was captured so beautifully both in the wonderful book, movie, "A Beautiful Mind" and in his Nobel Prize acceptance speech. He in essence proclaimed "Cor Super Ratio" [to quote from a paper by Bruce Di Marsico], "The Heart over the Mind," or happiness over beliefs, no matter how stubborn such beliefs might be, and delusions are indeed beliefs, however they may be abetted by a malfunctioning cerebral neuro-biology. He had shone the light of his joy into the darkness of the pharmaceutically created brain disorder and had affirmed the truth of his own happiness beyond the reach of mismatched synapses and "twisted" brain cells. I experienced the elation of my own awe in the light of his bravery and devotion to his joy and was inspired to move forward with seeking to know more about the truth of my happiness.

- Beach Plums. One morning my wife and I emerged from Peconic Bay—she after her morning swim and I after my morning jog in the bay. The area is populated with high dunes and salt water ponds and marshes with dense thickets of dune grass, brambles, and lush vegetation that has learned to live in the demanding conditions of sand and water. That morning, across the expanse of beach we spied a figure moving in and out of the dunes, hunched over and carrying a small bucket. Drying off, we became entranced with the ballet this figure traced as he carefully threaded his way through the crowds of flowers and blossoms, a collage of exquisite shapes and colors, a chorus of life moving to the unheard promptings of nature's inner metabolism, an endless symphony of growth and abundance.

  As we left the beach this figure emerged from the sandy forest on to the pathway that led to the parking area. We gladly gave into our desire to find out what he had been doing with such care and concentration. The figure, upon closer view, was a man in his late '70s or early '80s dressed simply in blue denim and light blue short sleeves, all leathery tan with a fisherman's cap and face awash with an ocean of wrinkles surrounding a vast, friendly smile and bright soft eyes. He warmed to our inquiries and happily informed us that what he was doing was gathering beach plums, a fruit only slightly larger than a grape, deep blue with streaks of green, a characteristic, he explained, of their being picked just short of full ripeness. But, he nodded knowingly, this was the time to pick them and allow them to ripen for about three days to a week. Then, he noted with enthusiasm, his grandchildren would carry on an old family tradition and turn them into a rare jam that has consistently brought blue ribbons at the local county fairs.

  Few now know the lore of beach plums he asserted with pride. You have to know how to find them and, he added with a chuckle, they have a propensity for growing in the neighborhood of poison ivy. That explained the careful balletic motions as he negotiated the thickets where the precious fruit grew in isolated, well defended splendor. One false move and I'd be up to my nose in rashes, he laughed, but after all these years his body was trained to arch like a dancer and insinuate itself deep into the bramble castle of the beach plum kingdom. He had learned the art of beach plum gathering from his grandfather who had in turn learned it from his, and so on back in time. With a twinkle of his eye he showed off his purple plunder: several dozen plums resting upon one another like sleeping puppies, shiny with the morning dew, blue blooded captives destined to be cooked and reduced to an imperial brew of unsurpassed succulence.

This wizard of the dunes turned and ambled spryly to his old pickup, the precious bucket swinging gingerly in one hand. We stood in silent awe watching his departure, marveling at his joy and spontaneous elation. The electric quality of his happiness resonated with our own feelings made effervescent from our thirty five minutes or so in the crisp early morning water. How generous nature can be with its revelations. Each moment is a page unfolding. With unrestrained pleasure we added the beach plum and the gnome who gathered them to the book of life's treasures, anxious to impart to our grandchildren the tale of those inhabitants of the magical land whose gentle sleep in the cradle of their vines was lovingly interrupted by the gentle tug of this enchanted reaper, bringing them to a Holy Communion of shared nurturance, a taste of which had been imparted to us one beautiful morning, once upon a time.

• *UPON THE DEATH OF MY DEAREST FRIEND, NICKI.*

The eyes said it all! They watched me with such intensity, such focus. In that moment of seeing one another was summed up every instant of our mutual lives together. His arrival as but a handful of fluff, a seemingly impossible frame too tiny to hold life. Yet from the very first instant of our encounter, life was manifest in unabashed abundance. No holding back, no coyness. Out it came, plain, direct, overflowing with excitement and curiosity. God, was I privileged to be both a witness to and a partner in that living arc of tireless, indomitable wonder, that intrusion of angelic abandon into my life.

Now at first, I did not recognize this. At first, I held back, kept him at arms length. But he was patient. He pursued me with a sensitivity to my reticence, but with a persistence that contained a knowingness about me. Soon, very soon, I capitulated and declared undying love. And, oh, he was such fun to love! That's what came flooding into my mind today, though that understanding had always been there without ever having been articulated quite that way. It came today, this, the day of his passing, the day I had to surrender this precious barely three pounds of passionate, turbulent joy. It was swelteringly hot and I went into the bay after burying my tiny friend in a bag filled with flowers. The water was cool, refreshing and I moved in it up to my neck. There was a great pause inside of me. And then in a torrent out came the most curious combination of laughter and tears that shook my frame and made a wide burst of circles on the surface of the calm, evening water. God, he was such fun to love and my mind was flooded with such delightful memories of his playfulness, the utterly engaging way he had of being with me. How he would run with his brother on the beach with such speed and aplomb, changing directions in seemingly impossible acrobatic maneuvers of surpassing agility. His little face would be screwed up in a mock seriousness, his tiny eyes would look at you from their very corners, inviting you to join in the fun, defying you to try and catch him. And oh I would chase him and laugh and thunder at my inability to capture my little furry rocket. But using my own guile I would sometimes succeed and scoop him up like a football, hold him up to my face and gaze into his sparkling eyes. He was the very soul of playfulness, the joy of motion. You could feel the elation of life moving musically in his limbs, the exquisite little squeal and whimper he would make when you folded his little head under your chin and just held him tight, but ever so gently tight.

Take that and multiply it and so much more unsaid in this brief testimony by thirteen years. He gladdened my heart on countless occasions, not merely by acrobatics and all the scintillating dynamisms of his puppy period, his middle age, and his ever vivacious growth that did not dim, even in those final moments. Yes I treasure all that and repeat it endlessly in my mind's eye as I type these words. But the deepest treasures were the quiet moments. Every evening at a certain time he would walk up to where I was sitting, gently tap me with his paw and then turn around, leg gracefully uplifted in anticipation of my picking him up and placing him close by my side. There he would stay, every day of his life. From the chair we would eventually find our way to the bed where he would fold himself in my arms and we would dream our separate dreams in a shared embrace.

God how I laughed in the water as the truth of this revelation soaked fully into my awareness. *My little teacher*, the one who led me by the nose to fully enjoy being with him in each and every interaction we had. Life has been so generous. Love has come to me from so many sources: parents, brother, wife, children, friends, a man who lovingly left me his legacy of unsurpassed wisdom about the truth of my happiness. Truly my cup runneth over and joy is my meat and my sustenance forever. But, oh my friends, the laughter that came as I realized that this barely gravitationally challenged bundle of furry defiance and audacious love had tutored me in ways that I shall probably never fully understand and to the degree that I do understand them, never fully share with anyone because the truth and the implications of what I have already come to know run far too deep into my soul for this age to bear with an open mind. It has been said that the most incredible three pounds that we know of in the universe up to this point is the human brain. Who am I, humble plebian soul that I am to challenge such obvious insight and wisdom. But yet, in the teeth of those who will smile indulgently, if they are generous, or yawn with cynicism about yet another maudlin animal tale, if they are less generous, in the teeth of that, I say again, I found the most precious three pounds I have ever known to be a tiny dog named Nicki.

Yes, *all that was contained in that final look as life passed out of him.* While every fiber in my being would strain against the inevitability of that moment, the breadth and depth of the gift that last look represents to me simply vibrates in my soul, fills every pore of my awareness and remains with me now as strong as in that moment and shall so remain until my own eyes close upon the broad and beautiful vistas of this world and upon the remaining faces of those I love. Here's a final shout in praise of love, of joy, in praise of my friend Nicki, 1986-1999. I shall seek you out oh delight of my soul, and strain to hear your welcoming bark if death is as I suspect but a bluff and bullying shadow.

NATURE

- This morning as I was walking away from the beach, I heard a sound of unearthly magnificence above me. I looked up to see two swans in flight. They seemed to stretch forever into the brilliant sunshine of the early morning sky, and fortunately were only about thirty feet or less above my head. This allowed me to drink in the incredible beauty of their symmetry as they moved overhead. First, they were locked in a confluence of motion with one bird just slightly leading the other so as to leave the absolute minimum amount of room for the wings of both to move in marvelous synchrony. Their bodies were as straight as the arches of a cathedral. All seemed effortless and pure joy in flight. However, beyond the startling visual presentation, there was above all the symphony of harmonics that they sang to each other in an unremitting chain of seamless sounds. What was so remarkable was the intense intimacy of their songs to one another. It was not an intensity of volume, but an intensity that manifested in the unbelievable closeness of the harmonies. If you were to imagine it as measures of music or as a graph of the amplitude of each chorus, what struck you was the unimaginable precision with which one set of sounds succeeded the other leaving what seemed like no room at all between the two sets and at the same time not in any way stepping on the sounds of the partner. Seamless is the word that fits, and yet the clarity of each song was unmistakable despite the virtual similarity of sounds. Still, there was a subtlety of difference that made the listening all the more enjoyable. The best description that comes to mind is that of two exquisitely tuned and acoustically sensitive harmonicas. They gave out their sounds with tones of perfect pitch and modulation, yet in no way was there the slightest sense of it being robotic or machinelike. Rather there was the sensitivity and emotional splendor of a concert pianist or concert violinist, a synergy of sound and love mixed with the irrepressible verve of life and the enjoyment of existence in the moment to the fullness of whatever it might mean to be these two creatures, locked in a moving arc of endless mutual devotion and trailing the sounds of that loving mutuality behind them, echoing into the treetops, the dunes, the sand, and the very marrow of my own heartfelt gratitude to have been at that time and place to behold the sacrament of their presence in the world.

• Near my home is a gorgeous salt water pond surrounded by dunes and high grass. It is the home to swans, ducks, loons, cranes, seagulls, crows and an endless assortment of interesting living things. At one point nearest to the beach that separates it from the larger body of water, Peconic Bay, the pond has an estuarial channel that allows it to change its volume of water as a sort of tidal basin. This channel's bed is lined with small stones ranging in size from grains of sand to a golf ball, with a vast majority averaging about the circumference of a robin's egg. When the water begins to flow either way in or out, the proximity of the stones to the shallow surface creates an endless pattern of ribbed and geometric forms that constantly come into being and alter at each moment as they move along out of your sight to blend with the stillness of the pond or, at low tide, with the sometimes stillness, sometimes turbulence of the bay. To look directly upon the surface is to become entranced with the glory of the movement. Also, it is so incredibly quiet at that spot that you can hear the sound of the moving stream, a sound that is ever so elusive in its quality. Every few seconds or so, it gives out the tiniest gurgle or whistle, sounds of such a beautiful evanescent quality that they defy all verbal encapturement.

What this stream means to me varies each time that I behold it. But on occasions, the thought came to me that these endless variations of patterns that are formed on the surface of the water, for all their complexity and constant alteration, are very much like our unhappy beliefs. They inhabit the mere surface of our being and move swiftly, carried along by the contingencies and laws of time and space and leaving no actual trace on the true element that allows their existence in the first place: the water itself. Try as you may, when you cast your gaze upon that moving stream, you inevitably find your vision being moved in the direction of the flow and what you see in the distance is all of that surface intensity of vortices and whorls slowing down and smoothing out into the calm surface of deeper waters where all of the patterns fade and meld into a calming, seamless, undisturbed surface. For me in the instance of observation I am describing, that represented the truth of our happiness. The business and apparent intractability of some of our unhappy ways of believing are but eddies in the true stream of our existence. Beneath the surface is the medium of our contentment, that truth in which we have our being, our happiness. As we allow ourselves to understand this, then, the whorls and gyres of surface beliefs flow swiftly into the larger body of equanimity. All gives way to the depths of bliss and joy. So allow yourself to imagine that you are breathing comfortably and as you exhale, you cast upon the surface of the swift flowing waters of time in motion, any unhappiness that comes to mind. Just let it mate with any particular configuration that you see spontaneously appear on the moving surface. Watch as it flows away, breaking up and joining with other patterns and ultimately dissolving into the tensionless body of truth in happiness just a little further downstream. Become one with that surface and then as you feel comfortable, allow yourself to move into its depths. Feel the comforting sense of being buoyant and exhilarated by the feeling of all of you immersed in your joy and yet completely free to move about in it as it pleases you. Stay with the feelings and then when it seems appropriate, come to your present awareness and record your experiences.

• I came upon a tree branch that has been totally washed and shaped; a tube-like object in the shape of a flute, with holes in it somewhat like a flute would have. Slightly covered with sand, near the stream's edge. Imagine the wind blowing through this water and sand shaped flute, singing sweetly of the wonder of being shaped by one's joy if one gives oneself over to it. The sounds that will come from you will be the hymns and harmonies of happiness and gratitude.

• There is a tree, swept by the wind, a fir tree, bent away from the water, its limbs stretched backwards, like arms held aloft so that the wind can be fully felt. Its pine nettles are different from leaves; they are more densely bunched than leaves usually are. Additionally, there is a different sound when wind moves leaves. A rustling sound is heard than can be wonderfully complex. Here the sound is as if a thousand tiny sticks were shaking and colliding, making more a swooshing sound, as if you held up a broom and whirled it around over your head, but with much more dimension and depth of harmony. There is a sense of the thickness of the wind and the thickness of the sound when you listen, like a great harp, sensitive to the slightest tremor or strongest gust. As you run your fingers over the bark of the tree there is the dual sense of its being so delicate and yet so strong. You know that the roots of the tree must run very deep beneath the sand's surface and hinge on some unknown, unseen point that holds it fast over all the years and storms. Despite its bending in the wind's direction, it does not yield its place and always draws strength from the same hidden source. Our happiness has those qualities. We will shape ourselves in the fashion of the times in which we live, bend in the direction of the cultural winds and storms, but never do we release our hold on what makes us be what we are, our freedom in being happy, that point of singular truth that roots us in deep beneath the shifting sands of any cultural context and from which we draw the sap of joy and equanimity unendingly.

- I came across a pine cone somehow cut cleanly in half leaving the structure of the interior exposed. You could see with concrete clarity how the pine core issued from an apparently solid base and gradually funneled out to form chamber-like flutes that comprise the bulb of the cone itself. There was more than the satisfaction of mere curiosity when gazing upon the pine cone. It was as if something normally hidden, the generative core, the secret middle, the cozy center of this entity was now open to be seen. A feeling of shared intimacy came over me as I gazed upon it, a sense that the symmetries of our inner lives are a thing of beauty; that they come out of the oneness of the base of all, out of our being in freedom and happiness; that they arch outwards into the world to express themselves in the architecture of our feelings and behaviors; that we are at root a oneness that enjoys playing at multiplicities in the world.

- I met a two foot section of a maple tree, about ten inches in diameter. The bark had been totally worn away so that it was naked to the morning sun, burnished by the elements and bronzed into the softest buff tones. It had the appearance of such delicacy that one felt that to touch the surface would produce the effect like the finest talcum powder, a degree of softness and smoothness unimaginable until you actually let the kinesthetic gap between your fingertip and the surface of the wood be gently closed. A sense of gratitude for the generosity of nature in its apparent random creations welled up in me. So much is there for us to enjoy and marvel at. We need only meet it with our own experience to find some explosion of beauty set off by the lovely collusion of the world and our openness to make of it a gallery of unending delights.

• This morning as I turned back onto the main road from a path leading from one end of my lengthy daily walk, I was joined by a black Labrador retriever who simply galloped across a meadow and settled into a pacing trot ahead of me. Not a sound was exchanged, but all was in the movement of bodies and the back long glances that were thrown my way by a radiant face and sparkling eyes. Through a series of licks, nods and shimmering, electric body motions, I was initiated into a silent conspiracy to accompany my dark friend in an exploration of the side of the road and ultimately of the beach we reached in about ten minutes of walking. She led the way, knowingly, zigging and zagging for side explorations into the woods, with occasional stops for some intense olfactory explorations of mysterious piles of leaves and brambles, the significance of which escaped my limited knowledge of the priorities of her world. Despite all these side trips, she maintained an easy distance ahead of my "racewalking" body. When we moved out upon the open space of the beach, her intensity increased with every step. The brightness of the sun and the verve of a gentle wind were an inspiration for her to race wildly to the water and just barely splash her feet into the still chilled February bay. She turned and jumped and gamboled with unabashed elation, kicking up sand, turning, and reeling from time to time to make sure that I was still on her trajectory until we reached a stream that joined a salt lake and the bay. Here we turned and started our return. I looked at her paw prints in the sand near the water's edge. Some had already been eroded by the action of the tides, others, stood boldly challenging the water's action as if they would be impervious to erasure. But a look at the smooth surface that surrounded our footprints gave evidence that that was not to be the case. For, how many feet, paws, claws and other appendages of life forms have marked the surface of this place over countless years. My dark friend was not in any way concerned with the permanence of her physical impact upon this place. No, she was totally into the dynamic beauty of feeling all dimensions of her sensory existence now. Instantly I was yoked with her in the awe of being fully into the wonder of the moment. Though it might bring different things flowing from our differing natures, still the underlying commonality of shared participation in the glory of living together this magical present was exhilarating.

We left the beach and at a certain point in the return journey, my dark friend tossed her head and looking me full in the face, turned and scampered off into the woods no doubt on a path back to her home. It was a blessing to have had the time with her that I had. Gratitude welled up in me at the marvel of such a spontaneous and fortuitous meeting. There was such an ease in communing with me for forty minutes or so and an equal ease in parting. We had known the maximal joy from our mutual journey. It was something absolutely whole and entire unto itself. Nothing was required in addition. We met in happiness and parted the same way. I am pleased and full of gratitude to say that my black friend has joined me on many other occasions. Always she seems to come from nowhere full of boundless energy and joy. We mesh immediately in that conspiracy of intimate play and we part as easily and effortlessly. Indeed that is the circle of joy, happiness in the beginning, happiness in the end, so that it does not really matter whether something is an end or a beginning. What is always true, always your companion, always the sinew and bone of your being is your happiness.

• One day when spring had suddenly broken the grip of winter and the temperature rose into the seventies, while the wind remained strong and gusty, I sat at the edge of the sea and watched the waves breaking endlessly into foam. What instantly came to mind was an image of the waves like fingers playing on the giant keyboard of the great stretch of beach. The breaking of the waves into foam were like white knuckles rising and falling at maximum tempo driven by the wind into a ceaseless sonata. The sun glistening off the top of each wave highlighted how the "fist" of each wave folded down into a thousand digits, all created and recreated constantly in profligate profusion. The sound was of the incredible harmonies of nature weaving endless symphonies like vast throngs cheering in constant elation singing the hosannas of existence out of their boundless gratitude for being alive in joy.

• There is the sound of a bird, unseen, giving out a particular call, echoing through the woods in early morning. Not the prettiest or the most melodic call, but the most unusual, somehow insistent, catching my ear with that edge of invitation. But to what? I walk further, then the call comes again. Could it be the same bird or just a random fellow of the same species making that call? But the sense of it talking to me increases. What does it know that it is trying to urge me to understand? What do I know that we could have in common? Ah yes. My joy, its joy. What a gift to be so exotically reminded once again.

• WINGS AND WEATHER.
Six A.M. My body moves with increasing smoothness of rhythm through the humid, friendly air. As usual, the initial stiffness of limbs

fades into a gentle lubricating sensation that fades even more as the scrumptious activity of mind and imagination bubble and boil with excitement. I am jogging, yes, but with even more intensity, I am thinking. Thinking in a free flow of associations that come faster than memory can record them. It is as if the universe were generously pouring from the pitcher of creativity into the human vessel, the neuronal bowl of my brain. The precious liquid sways perilously in my recall, with delicious rivulets of inspiration pouring over the sides into temporary forgetfulness. It is okay to balance the momentum of the moment with the desire to get home and record some of what is taking place.

Then a car passes along beside me and my attention is drawn for some reason to the road, to a particular spot the tires have just passed over. There, on the ground is something extraordinary. I race past it, stop and circle back. Two gorgeous butterflies, joined together, one in some ecstasy of passive receptance, quiet still, trancelike; the other, in full glory, wings spread, gently, ever so slowly waving, attentive in some inexplicable way. A moment of the most intense connection and creation is taking place, there on the asphalt, denying with the assurance of the power of creation any contingency or danger. There is perhaps something there that I do not yet know; my vision is to take them from the middle of the road to what I perceive is a safer place for this unfolding to evolve. I pick them up; there is no struggle or concern; the one lies soft and quiet, the other clings to my fingers; the recall of that sensation, the clutch, perhaps even, the knowing embrace, of something so tiny remains pungent on my skin as I write these words. Even more extraordinary, I stroke them lovingly with the barest touch that I can muster, no pressure at all in so far as I can sense this; the clutch remains steady, the gentle resting in the palm is a calm as ever. Could it be that they know in some superlative way what I am coming to know? There is a deep resonance; I place them in the lightest possible way in the concave hold of the limb of a tree. The tiny legs at first resist removal and then gently yield. It is time to move on. Tears of gratitude well up as I urge my body back into motion.

Then, a connection. It was one of the earliest theoreticians of chaos, in the most recent wave of post W.W.II thinkers, Edward Lorentz, who in 1963 came upon the revelation that most of reality is unpredictable, particularly, since he was researching in meteorology, the weather. The tiniest perturbation in the earth's atmospheric system can have colossal ramifications at a remove of many months and thousands of miles. His way of putting it, in paraphrase, was that *the flapping of a butterfly's wings in Hong Kong in May will determine the weather in Kansas in October.* Our happiness is like the gentle waving of that butterfly's wings; so apparently insignificant, so seemingly vulnerable as we live in the middle of the road facing at any moment the contingency of the heavy tread of society's, the culture's, nature's passing "vehicles"; yet, there is a knowing, that the loving perturbance of our happiness ripples outward, gathers momentum together with the cumulative verve of all those who live their happiness. Let us be grateful for that turbulence. The folks in Kansas could use the rain. Keep those wings flapping!

- ICE PANES:

This has been another mild winter thus far. However, this morning there was a strong frost on the grass as I looked out into my backyard. It was about seven o'clock and I was leaving the house to do my daily run on the beach. I noticed right away that although it was cold, the air was absolutely still; not a whisper of a breeze in the air. Also, it was a glorious day that was beginning; the sun was rising strong and bright, filled with the confidence of its growing power as Spring approached a little more than a month away on the calendar.

As I moved toward the beach from about two blocks away, I noticed that it looked unusual. The surface seen from that distance had strange marks upon it. They looked at that remove like sketch lines that an artist had roughed in while beginning a drawing. The slanting rays of the sun revealed what looked like a calm sea surface, but it was only when I actually ran up to the water that I took in the glory of what had happened.

The bay was covered for as far as I could see with a thin layer of ice that was clear enough to allow the color of the water to come through. This had happened because there had been no air movement at all, so that the water, being still all through the night, was able to form this opalescent skin that now shone in brilliant, ebullient tones in the light of the early sun.

That sun, however, had the effect of adding just enough warmth to the surface, so that even though the water was as still as it can get, there was the barest gentle motion in the bay that began to create cracks in the surface of this mighty canvas. The results were extraordinary. First, the cracks themselves created the most intricate patterns. I was reminded of graphs of the formidable processes of the basic metabolism of the universe, of the movement of basic particles, of the unfolding potentials of sound and light that I had seen in books and lectures over the years. Ah, perhaps here was revealed in an act of delightful whimsy all of Nature's most intimate secrets: the key to immortality; the formula for unlimited energy; the design for the capability to cruise effortlessly and in an instant throughout all the galaxies; the very sound of the sigh God made to bring the universe into being. All of it spread out for but an instant in the uncovering rays of the Sun.

Standing fixed and transfixed at the very edge of the water, I was then treated to a sound like the sound of a thousand tiny wings, something I had heard in a huge hedge that housed hundreds of tiny birds once while visiting Jamaica. What was happening was that large pieces of the frozen bay were being moved ever so slowly on top of other large pieces that remained stationary. The gentle action of the water caused these chunks of "canvas" to slide with eerie precision toward the shoreline. Soon they reached the sand where they continued to move. As I looked to my right and left to see what was happening along the whole stretch of beach, I was greeted with an incredible sight. These magnificent shards of wafer thin ice were coming ashore in the most delicate invasion of grace and wonder. As they moved further inland over the sand, their leading edges were refined by contact with that wet, subtly abrasive surface into a long corridor of arches of varying sizes. At the same time, the sun revealed the ice to be a complex, textured surface of what appeared to be an infinite number of snowflake designs all clustered together in a crystal vein of endless variations. I moved back slowly so as not to impede the motion of these frozen stain glass windows, designed by a canny mixture of chance and intelligence into a cathedral of momentary splendor. I allowed myself to break off a small piece of the arch nearest to me. It crunched with the utmost delicacy of a baked phyllo leaf and then dissolved into a fading translucence in the palm of my hand until there was nothing but tiny rivulets of liquid streaming over the corners of my fingers.

As the last drops disappeared from my hand I looked about the large bowl of sea, earth and sky growing ever more warm and radiant. The arches were now fading quickly into the sand, the ice yielding to the critical leap from crystal to liquid dictated by the laws of physics. The canvas disappeared and the bay resumed its more normal, though still enchantingly beautiful configuration. Waves of wonder crested inside me and flowed in the form of tears from my eyes. There was such gratitude for this moment. Had I been but a mere few moments late, the whole panoply of beauty would have faded and remained, to me at least, a dish untasted, a song unsung. Yet, I happened upon this symphony of crystalline motions and was a privileged witness to its unsurpassed unfolding. This moment, this joy of bliss in the now. It is a memory, but one that forms one of the most splendid stones in the monument of my own experience, my own cathedral that stretches in my imagination and my joy to the utmost edges of the universe where it joins with the chorus of all others into the hosannas sung with everlasting gratitude for the gift of happiness and the capacity to love life and to treasure such moments as this.

• LIGHT AND SHADOW

This morning I awoke and sat up in bed; leaning back on my pillow I was struck at the way the landscape outside my window suddenly was aglow with a light of surpassing beauty. It was about 7 o'clock and the dazzling display lasted for about two or three minutes perhaps. Then, it dimmed and disappeared leaving a gray and darkening sky behind. There was no way to fully express the experience of beholding that light; it was as if everything stood absolutely still and even my breath was suspended. Obviously, I did not want it to fade, but fade it did. I did not control it. It was a gift of nature either grasped or missed without apology.

What occurred to me in its wake was that there was a relation between the light and the shadowy grayness that followed when clouds obscured it. Goodness how deeply I preferred the light; how absolutely at ease and in full clarity were my thoughts and feelings as they rested in it. By contrast, the gray that followed it was not welcome, nor did it provide as comfortable a vessel for my good feelings to ramble about in. Now of course the world is just the way it is. My feelings do not have to be creatures of the changing moods of the weather. No, that is all simply interpretation. What did open up to me as a helpful metaphor was that despite the apparent grayness of the day and the disappearance of the light, the light still existed beyond the clouds that obscured it. So it is with our happiness, which is our fundamental light. It is always there ready to illuminate and enliven our being. However, we create the clouds that obscure it, we create the grayness that serves as a lesser illumination. Then, often we mourn the passing of the light as if it had been taken from us in the same way that the laws of physics working on the earth's surface altered the landscape for me from light to shadow. The truth, the profoundly good news is that we "cloud up" our experience with our beliefs in the necessity of unhappiness and then we become even more unhappy when we have to live our lives in the gray, sallow haze that is whatever light is allowed to remain in our experience. Things can grow very dark that way until we are in the deepest midnight of despair about ever seeing the light again. But we have only to affirm and make real through a "realization" the truth about our happiness—that it is who we are and always will be despite efforts to cloud our minds to this reality. Then, in an instant, the light of our joy breaks through, stuns us with its instant clarity, penetrates to the very marrow of our awareness and gladdens us without end.

• THE TREE

It was a rare trip to the ocean beach. I never frequent the ocean beaches at all during the summer months, and do so rarely even in the off season. This is primarily because I am so taken with the wonderful beaches that border Peconic bay. But all the circumstances lined up like the signs on an astrological chart: it was a brilliant sunny day; there was little wind; I had to be near the ocean beach on an errand; I was grumbling internally about some reversal the world had delivered to me and thought the ocean a proper place to affirm the passion of my not liking the train of events at that time. So shortly before eleven o'clock in the morning, I stepped foot on the vast open spaces of the ocean beach and traveled boldly right up to the edge of the fading waves. I made a sharp turn to the right and walked a parallel track along the parabolic edges of the rolling waves.

At first, I stayed pretty much with my grumbling affirmations and then gradually let myself sink into the synesthesia of sound, motion, glittering sunlight, salt-sea smell, caress of a gentle wind, the occasional crunch of seashells under my feet. There was a rhythm in all this, not unfamiliar in its pattern, since I experienced something like it every day at the bay; but here it was magnified exponentially into a torrent of sensations, a veritable galaxy of explosions on the palate of my perceptions. Enchantment twined its serpentine fingers through every sensory pore of my being. Snatches of grumbling would well up from time to time. And then I saw a tree standing like a naked person in the midst of an endless vista of fine sand, empty of any vegetation as far as the eye could see, except for the dune grass that accumulated some density as you moved landward far away from the shore.

It was scruffy, scrawny, no more than ten feet high, obviously of the pine family. As I approached this anomaly standing in sorry resplendence, the sense of displacement and implausibility increased. Ah, ha, I said to myself, it is some kind of ruse. Someone, or ones, decided for reasons unfathomable, to take this wooden body that had once been a tree in some respectable place probably not too far away, and plant it in the middle of nowhere on this stretch of beach. I was almost upon it, and though the wind was weak, I had a premature confidence that it would go tumbling over into the silence of a horizontal eternity with one minor shove of my foot. Thus would I defeat whatever intentions those parties unknown might have had in creating such a travesty. This tree deserved better than to accumulate the ongoing scorn of passersby who would immediately see through the pathetic attempt at verisimilitude. So imagine my surprise when stepping right up to it, my confident surmise was met with a sound rebuttal as my foot met with a solid unyielding trunk. It did not budge. I grabbed hold of one of the broken branches and attempted to shake it. It would not move. I examined it closely. There was not a chance in the world that this was a live growing entity. Its bark was faded; there were no real limbs, just broken hints of former life. The base of the tree was partially uncovered to reveal how the root system evidently was indeed dispersed deeply in the sand. My God, I thought, someone truly troubled themselves to plant this dead tree in the sand so that it would have a solid base. But why? A dead tree clinging to life. For some reason the whole panoply of incongruities suddenly brought me to deep and vibrant laughter. A dead tree deeply rooted in the sand, hoping for the best. That phrase "hoping for the best," flashed into my mind with the tides of mirth. I recalled some years ago hiring a painter/handyman who went about doing repairs with such a serious demeanor. When he came upon something that he evidently thought required some substantial redoing, he would present it to me with a sense of urgency. At times I would agree, and at other times I would resist his importuning and suggest that he simply try less drastic or even merely cosmetic approaches to the problem. Then he would look at the area to be repaired, look at me and shake his head seriously saying: "Well so okay fine, I will do what you want and we will just hope for the best." We would then exchange almost conspiratorial glances as if to say:

"we both know that this is not going to work, but we will sort of agree to act as if it might." He would then nod his head, purse his lips a bit and sort of mutter half to himself, "yes, well okay, so we will hope for the best."

The laughter continued in little driblets of chuckles as I walked around the tree, catching myself reproducing the stance and demeanor of my dour repairman. A great admiration welled up in me for this firmly rooted corpse. As I walked away, I continued to give it backward glances and wonder how long it would withstand the formidable elements of wind and tides. It occurred to me that my even having a momentary sense that a tree could grow in that spot was totally incongruous. Nothing can grow in that sand that near to the water. But, yet, this once living wiry pine had all the outward appearances of being there somehow naturally. Its lifeless roots stretched deep into the lifeless sand, a confluence of deadness producing the appearance of the drama of life. Yet, how many trees in the forest have been so caressed with glances and pondered with the wondering impossibility of it all? Not bad, not bad at all. But even living trees must ultimately surrender their grip on the soil. This wooden shell was in the same position. It had been given a second chance, however mechanical and crude had been its jocular transplantation. The sand would defeat its lifeless grip at some point in time, but so what? Our purchase on the world is no different, so there is no need to gloat over the discovery of its hopeless, "hoping for the best." The best is not in the grip, nor in the length of our time in holding that grip against the world, the best is in the moment joyfully lived for that is what the grip provides us with the opportunity to experience. So hurrah for that tree that only simulated life. Its presence was enough to give me a moment of joy while life was yet left in my grip.

• THE LOON

Well, you would think that one dead tree making believe it was alive and hoping for the best would be gift enough for a mid-day walk on the ocean beach. But as that tree faded into the distance, I decided finally to plant myself in the sand and simply gaze at the feast of sounds and sensations spread out before me on this endless banquet table. This day had shown me in a number of ways how the world has its own designs and my desires are not necessarily priorities on its list of wants to be fulfilled. This was hardly a new revelation. The rolling vastness of the sea seemed to confirm my musings. It was here to be seen if seeing it is what I am open to. If not, then it does not change or desist in its own gravitational agenda. The decision to join for a time in the labor of its endless unfolding is mine alone.

So I joined, and as I was paying attention to one particular quadrant of ocean just in front of me, I became aware of a black object floating on the surface. There was absolutely nothing else in sight. No boats, no birds, no people, nothing but the roiling surface of the green giant. But again, there it was, now coming into focus as a gull, no, a duck, still no, but there, a loon. Unmistakable in its streamlined body and slender arrow like head, with a typical circle of white below the neck. Even on this day when the ocean is merely lolling toward shore, the creature was bobbing around vigorously on the surface. I was transfixed with the sight of it, as it skillfully negotiated the moving hills and valleys with liquid ease. Then, as loons will do, it dove beneath the surface and disappeared, probably in search of some fish. I did not flinch in my fixed stare at that spot on the ocean's surface. I had been more acquainted with loons on the bay, where the surface is much calmer normally and their signature calls to one another would echo out over the bowl of this more restricted body of water. They would dive and after a moment or so, would reappear, repeating this ritual of search over and over.

So, I waited for this solitary loon to surface. Time passed, a minute, two, three, four, I don't know exactly how long in all. I didn't want to check my watch because I did not want to lose the angle of sight and risk missing his resurfacing. But now, it occurred to me that resurfacing was not an automatic thing guaranteed to the loon. Beneath the surface were other creatures of equal or superior cunning and agility whose own purposes might preclude that loon from ever reappearing. No matter, though, I was rooting for the loon. I wanted to see that sleek body pop up just once more. But, wait, there again is something I want that may not be granted by the caprice of nature. The loon and I shared the same conditions of life. It was not given to me to bring into being all that I have wanted in my life; this loon faced the same truth. Still, I waited as more time passed. Nothing to be seen. Carefully, I altered the angle of my sight to sweep the area in as precise a way as I could, while still keeping the same general orientation. Nothing. Gradually, I arose from my position in the sand, keeping my glance steadily focused on the magic patch of sea. But, too much time had passed, I thought. This loon is not coming back from the briny depths.

Reluctantly I relaxed my gaze and turned to retrace my steps. One less loon, one less wish granted in an ocean of wanting. One could drain the sea of all desires and live upon the parched earth of cynicism. Certainly, I had known periods in my life when I had done just that. But because like King Canute, I don't control the tides and the seas, shall I refrain from the verve of attempting to embrace all that I can? No, the tree had reminded me of the gift of this moment's potential to be at peace and happy with what is given and with what is taken away. I did not have to celebrate my losses, but they did not represent the juice of my existence. There will be many more things ungranted before I join that tree in the shadowy splendor of remembrance. Hardly had I finished the thought when I paused, took a deep breath and happily discovered that I was suddenly in love with that moment and gratitude was flowing in the arteries of my soul. I picked up my pace in a swelling pride of homecoming. Something prompted me to glance backward in final tribute to my absent comrade lost at sea. Then, there, right out there, first perhaps merely wishful thinking, but then absolutely and clearly; there was the loon bobbing merrily on the surface. What lungs! What do you know a Hollywood ending. I danced my way back to the car with an appropriate bow to the tree that is not a tree and left the beach singing.

- RADIANCE IN WINTER.

This morning, close to the anniversary of the death of Bruce Di Marsico, I had a special experience that evoked his memory. It was early in the morning, just at daybreak. The sky was partially overcast but there was an opening in the east through which the first rays made a magnificent entry into the dome of sky over the bay. I stopped at the crest of the dunes some forty feet above the beach and then caught sight of the ways the light played on the tops of the tallest trees. For a moment I was simply stopped, all motion seemed to cease and then that almost unbearably beautiful light brought back to my mind the light I had seen shortly before Bruce's death.

Its qualities are that of utter softness, a kind of silken hue of the utmost delicacy. One gets a sense that if you were bathed in that light that you would become completely translucent yourself; that you would find yourself floating through an atmosphere like the softest down, caressed by a shower of light beams having the characteristic of a gentle snow shower, only without any sensation of cold. Although it was absolutely quiet and still, no wind at all, this radiance seemed to be accompanied by a sound. This is indeed difficult to explain but the light has a tone, a resonance, a definite acoustic dimension. If pressed to describe it further, it was like a continuous note in a huge chorus of voices that seemed to shift subtly and effortlessly through a continuum of sinuous vocal alterations.

A deep and abiding lightness and elation invaded every pore of my sensory awareness. I was transfixed by this light; then, as suddenly as it had appeared, it faded in tinkling sparkling tones until it was fully replaced by the normal robust intensities of morning sunlight. I was filled with a wonderful sense of Bruce's presence and a connection and camaraderie that was visceral and real to me. As I moved down the dune and onto the beach to begin my run, this feeling accompanied me and my whole sensorium was drenched with a perfect sense of meaning and equanimity.

- SEEING THE WIND

This morning was extraordinary. Just a few days before Christmas and there is a strong, balmy wind with the temperature somewhere near sixty. The sky is heavily laden with storm clouds, yet no rain has fallen and so there is still time to take my usual morning run on the beach with my ever present companion Wonder, a mixed breed dog who has that name because of some special qualities he has in befriending other animals, especially one of our cats, Pie.

As I approach the beach, from the normal vantage point of dunes thirty to forty feet above, I notice an unusual mix of circumstances. The water is quite placid and flat despite a very strong wind. That seems to be because the wind is basically coming off the land and keeping the incoming water quiescent. Quiescent, that is, except for one magical difference. The strong shifting breezes are tracing patterns on the otherwise tranquil surface of the water. As I begin to jog the swift alterations in those patterns engage my eyes and I am taken up more and more fully into their dancing spontaneity. Most of all what strikes me is that by watching the patterns on the water, I can actually see the wind! When one of the round nosed waves comes rushing towards me on the surface, I know in an instant I shall feel the force of the wind making that wave. To see the endless variations of interacting crescents swirl and bump into each other is to be reminded of the effortless merriment and ceaseless play of dogs and children. The motion never stops and you are included in the game at every turn. Only now you know when you are going to be lovingly enveloped by these playful, normally invisible giants. It is another gift of revelation, another way to see the world, another secret lovingly unfolded if only for a brief time. Yet, once known it remains another stone of awareness in the structure of yourself, an edifice of unending possibilities, a work that bridges the gap of the ages between earth and sky, the visible and the invisible, what is known and what is now joyfully come to be known.

FINAL THOUGHTS

SOME FINAL THOUGHTS

Expect no further word or sign from me.
Your own will is whole, upright and free
And it would be wrong not to do as it bids you,
Therefore I crown and miter you over yourself.
Canto XXVIII, Purgatorio, Dante's Divine Comedy.

FINAL THOUGHTS

- Some people are unhappy about the prospect that *you* might be happy and *they* will not be. *You* have no "right" to be happy if that is something *they* feel they cannot have as well. Thus they fear your happiness because it reminds them of their failure or inability to be happy (as they experience it). They want you to fear your happiness as well as a source of their displeasure!

- If you try to be "good" instead of happy, you will probably become depressed. That is because at the core, happiness is for happiness alone, not for the sake of anything else, not for goodness, wealth, health, relationships etc. Otherwise, it would just be another occasion for failure, since according to the ABC's of happiness you do not control any of those things (health, wealth, relationships "goodness').

- Happiness is your ground state, the alpha and the omega of the truth of what it is like to be human, what it is like to be you. Think of it this way: if you were not blind but were blindfolded and then the blindfold was removed. What would you have to do to be able to see? That's right, nothing, absolutely nothing! Your ability to see was always available to you. It was the blindfold that prevented you from seeing, not any innate loss of vision. When the blindfold is taken way, you simply see. You don't have to learn anything, or gather any information, or be authentic, follow anybody's rules about getting permission to see, you just see! So it is with your happiness. Your beliefs are the blindfold. It is that and that alone which is your unhappiness. Once the blindfold is removed, that is, once the reasons for your unhappiness, your belief that you have to be unhappy, are removed, you simply are happy. No one else's permission or allowing is necessary. Yours alone is required. Your happiness is always available to you without any intervening limitations or reservations. Open your eyes and feast on that truth!

- Remember, your happiness (or unhappiness) *is the taste in your own mouth*! It is not generic, one size fits all for everyone. No one knows or could know the unique sense of what it feels like (tastes like) to be happy or unhappy in some specific way for you. You are the god creating the universe of your own beliefs and if you wish experiencing the uniqueness of your own experience of happiness.

- All unhappiness is a superstition, thus there is no purpose served by analyzing it beyond just identifying it! Why would you? Anything that is woven from unhappiness is just more unhappiness and there is nothing to learn except what you could already know, i.e., how unhappiness creates more unhappiness.

Happy Nut basic postulates:

- 1. *We are helpless/impotent.* Yes my friends, we are helpless in the sense that we do not control the world of B, the world of material causality. And leaving aside the possible role of a greater, benignly inclined intelligence rooted in Consciousness, we have to admit, rather, it controls you! The movement of the galaxies, the life time of the stars, the motion of tides, wind, weather, the movement of the earth's crust (especially relevant for all you West Coast people) the endless ways people deceive themselves through their beliefs in unhappiness and how they attempt to constrain you personally and through culture into those self same mythical prisons, the metabolic activity of your body, its slow (sometimes rapid) descent into senescence and ultimately the stasis of death. Science may indeed over the ages gain relative control over vast reaches of our material circumstances and all of this may be tinkered with or played with, sometimes in desperation, sometimes in whimsy, but never controlled **absolutely.** ***But who says you are supposed to be potent?*** Only the mythmakers with their beliefs in unhappiness. Take Mel Brooks advice; "just don't believe that!" Believing you have to be potent is just more unhappiness. Look, your "job" is simply to want what you want and change your mind as you find something you deem better to want. Getting what you want is irrelevant because it has nothing to do with your happiness. Hopefully, this statement will not seem as absurd at this point having done some of your Joywork, as it might have seemed initially. At first, you may only glimpse this ever so briefly and then expand your understanding of it as you mature in your practice of the Method; but, it is an awareness awaiting you and it is the moment of greatest liberation while you experience it. Wanting is just playing in the world to see what happens as you want what you want. I have not the slightest idea what the outcome of my or your wanting will be! I am being me and living me and that is my joy. Why you do what you do is not the question. Just know that you don't ***have to do*** what you do. You do it because that is what ***you want to do***!

- 2. ***We are ignorant.*** Also true. This really follows from the first Happy Nut postulate because part of the mythical imperative of being potent is knowing what we are supposed to do! Information amounts to control in the realm of "B" of the ABC's. Remember it is assumed that there are things to know, things that are required to understand *in order* to be happy! But folks, all the accumulated information of the ages has not added up to happiness has it? We will always be ignorant of what the mythmakers say is necessary in order to be happy, since the formula will always be tantalizingly just out of our grasp, around the next bend, at the next workshop, in the next scientific discovery, after the next promotion, when peace finally comes to humankind, when all the poor and hungry are fed, when "justice" reigns for all etc. In other words, whatever you or the culture makes it up to be. Let me now tell you the secret of happiness. Ready? Okay. *The secret of happiness is that it is not a secret!* It is who you *are* not something you acquire or become as the result of information you learn or stages you pass through or something you earn by being good or holy or simply first in line. All that is the belief that knowing, in the sense of information gathering is your salvation, i.e. the key to happiness. "Amen, amen I say unto you that unless you are willing to embrace your ignorance you will never experience the truth of your happiness." Sounds sort of biblical doesn't it. Now, obviously I am not exalting ignorance here but only disputing the notion that there are any informational requirements [usually in the form of allegiance to certain beliefs or cultural dictums] required in order for you to have permission to be happy. I have acknowledged elsewhere the utility of finding what information you may about the world so that you might achieve and realize as much of what you want as possible. It is simply that your success or lack of it in getting that information presents no impediment to your happiness.

- *So how do you let go of your unhappiness?* Well, first, one has to assume you actually want to do that (remember there are so many forms of unhappiness that are believed to be necessary and good for you to experience). Usually when things are not "working" for an individual, they then turn toward the possibility of changing or letting go of what is immediately in their behavioral experience that seems to be the cause of their unhappiness. Answer is simple. *Just stop being unhappy*. Ah, you say. Simplistic, impossible, ridiculous! We would all be happy if it were so simple. So what's the problem? Well it is that **YOU SIMPLY DO NOT BELIEVE YOURSELF!** You do not believe you are running you and therefore you do not believe that you have effective control over your emotional experience. Believing that you are so configured that other forces (unconscious, external in the realm of "B") dictate your emotional experience is why you don't stop being unhappy. You believe you have to be unhappy! *That you can't trust you* (You would not buy a used car from yourself!). The Option Method is simply to show you that you *are* in charge of your emotions! Once you know that, then you do not need the Option Method.

THE HAPPY NUT HAPPINESS LOGIC TREE 

Happiness Priority Exper/cise:

Purpose of the Exper/cise:

Essentially this is just another way to utilize and ask yourself the Option Method questions. The Option Method questions begin by asking you what you perceive to be causing you to be unhappy. The Happy Nut Happiness Logic Tree starts on the other end by asking you about what you perceive to be problematic about your happiness, but *only* in the context of when maintaining or attaining that happiness is raised as a problem. Obviously, we have no interest in questioning anyone's happiness unless they perceive there to be some issue around it that makes it problematic for them. The Logic Tree, then simply utilizes the OM questions in a particular, programmatic way to help clarify contexts in which happiness is experienced somehow as paradoxically potentially tinged with or limited by unhappy constraints. The focus here is to throw more light on how we create those constraints, those special requirements or permission giving devices, as I have called them, before we allow ourselves to be happy. We do this first, by limiting the contexts in which we allow happiness to be experienced and second by making our happiness subject to the rules of the realm of "B" and thus apparently out of our control. This will help to identify when we do this and point to how further use of the Option Method questions can clarify and release us from those constraining assumptions. This exper/cise gives a programmatic outline of how to challenge the pseudo logic of our beliefs in unhappiness. It comes at the end of the Workbook because it presumes some acquaintance with the Method and thus would serve you best after you have had some success in using it.

Be aware of the following distinction which follows from the logic of what you have already learned in this Workbook: anything in the world can at least theoretically be the occasion for affirming your happiness. Now, as we live our lives we certainly develop our own preferences as to what we consider the occasions we most likely are going to allow ourselves to be happy. As you grow in your happiness, you will undoubtedly find yourself expanding those preferences, i.e., set fewer and fewer limits on when it is okay to feel happy. Conversely, anything can be seen as the occasion for denying or limiting access to your happiness by creating permission giving devices that are the gateways guarded by your beliefs about when it is okay to feel happy and when unhappiness is required. In the first instance, to the degree you experience yourself in the moment according to the "C" perspective, whatever is selected as the occasion is not an essential requirement for your happiness but simply the context you have chosen to affirm that happiness. In the second, if you are following "B" of the "ABC's," the context is the essential ingredient that allows happiness and creating or controlling that context becomes the driving imperative in one's life.

We will start out with the following statement: HAPPINESS=

You will write in the box whatever happiness is for you in your life at this moment. Then you will answer a set of questions designed to help you clarify the degree to which you are operating in the realm of "B" or if you are affirming the truth of your happiness in the realm of "C." And please keep in mind that this exper/cise is not meant to be a complete description of your exploration of any issue but rather a guide to getting closer to your happiness on a consistent basis. If you feel you require more exploration, then utilize and ask yourself the Option Method questions to achieve as much clarity as you desire until you are feeling free enough to give yourself permission to be happy.

- Whatever you have written in the box, ["X" can represent anything put in the box, i.e., your husband's love or that of your son or daughter; health, money, fame, etc.] is that something over which you have control? **Yes** or **No**?

- If "**Yes**" then the only thing you could have written in the box would be a version of the statement we defined as "C" of the "ABC's." That is, "I do control the attitude that I create toward whatever the world may present to me at any given moment," or some close equivalent, i.e., "I am the sole arbiter of my emotional states etc." Most profoundly of all, perhaps, one could come to know that "Happiness = Who I am!" And remember, the ability to affirm that truth is really all you control. Thus you replace the notion of *pursuing* and *having* happiness as a transient, elusive quality that is always subject to being vetoed by the mysterious forces of the realm of "B," with *being* your happiness, where it represents a fundamental aspect of the *qualia* or actual core of the self, along with freedom. This gets you permanently out of the loop of unhappiness and the logic that exists when you search for happiness in the realm of "B."

- Now if you answered "**No**" to the first question, then whatever you have chosen belongs to the realm of "B" and you may be believing that your happiness is dependent upon your *having* whatever is in the box. In that case, there is a further set of questions that you can ask yourself to help get you to "C."

1/ Whatever is in that box, *who* decides that this is your happiness?

1/a If it is **you** then would you still want your happiness even though you didn't have "X"? [see below Section 2 if you answered that it is **not you** who decides that this is your happiness]

1/b If **Yes** then be happy now for you have found the truth about your happiness in this moment. *Now again **always remember** that you have the Method questions to explore and achieve as much clarity as you desire until you are willing to give yourself permission to be happy. So in this exper/cise when I note that you have found the truth about your happiness, I mean that as a potential given how you have answered the questions in this logic tree. As always, you are in your own hands and the act of allowing your happiness is born in your freedom and is inspired by your kindness, compassion , generosity and ultimately your gratitude toward yourself for affirming your happiness. As you do this more and more unconditionally in each and every moment you build the Attitude that we have spoken about that inclines you to remain happy as you greet each instant of life granted to you.*

1/c If **No**, then do you think it would mean anything at all about you were you to be happy despite not having "X"?

1/d If **No**, then be happy now for you have your happiness.

1/e If **Yes**, then are you saying that you believe that having your happiness in the face of (remember no one is asking you to be happy *about* your not having "X") not having "X" would demonstrate any or all of the following: a/ that your desire or love for "X" was not real, i.e., you did not really want what you say you wanted; b/ that you lack the desire, that you are incapable of love; that you lack strong enough desire to deserve to have what you want and therefore are a cold uncaring person or a lifeless weak person with no "authentic" "real" feelings; c/ that not to be unhappy in such an event would be a clear sign that you were out of touch with your "authentic" self and in deep "denial" of some negative feelings over which you have no control?

1/f If **No**, then be happy now for you have your happiness.

1/g If **Yes**, then be aware that your plea that you must have "X" in order to be happy falls on deaf ears in the realm of "B." The only ears with the compassion and power to hear and respond by giving you your happiness apart from anything you may desire in this world are *yours*! You can repeat your plea in an endless loop of pain and frustration, you can use whatever power strategies you know to get the world to give you what you want or you can embrace the truth about your happiness now and not be in dread as to whether those strategies will work. I invite you to do more of your *Joywork* and use the resources in this Workbook to achieve this priceless gift to yourself.

2/a If you answered above that you do **not** decide what is your happiness then who or what decides that "X" = happiness? No matter what the answer, keep asking the same question. Why? Because whatever you say decides that for you, the question can still be asked: "Then who or what decides/determines that the agency you describe as the authority over your happiness has the power to decide that?" In other words you end up with an infinite regression . And if you assert that God decides this, then ask yourself why God would put you in a position where happiness is impossible. Reread the chapter on God.

3/ If you change your mind and decide you *are* the one who decides this is your happiness, then reread the introduction to this exper/cise and then consider the "HAPPINESS =" equation again to see what you might put in the box now.

Let us test out our Happiness Logic Tree with a few hypothetical examples. Remember, what we are doing here is just another way of using the Option Method questions to get you to "C" so that you can live your joy each and every moment that you want to.

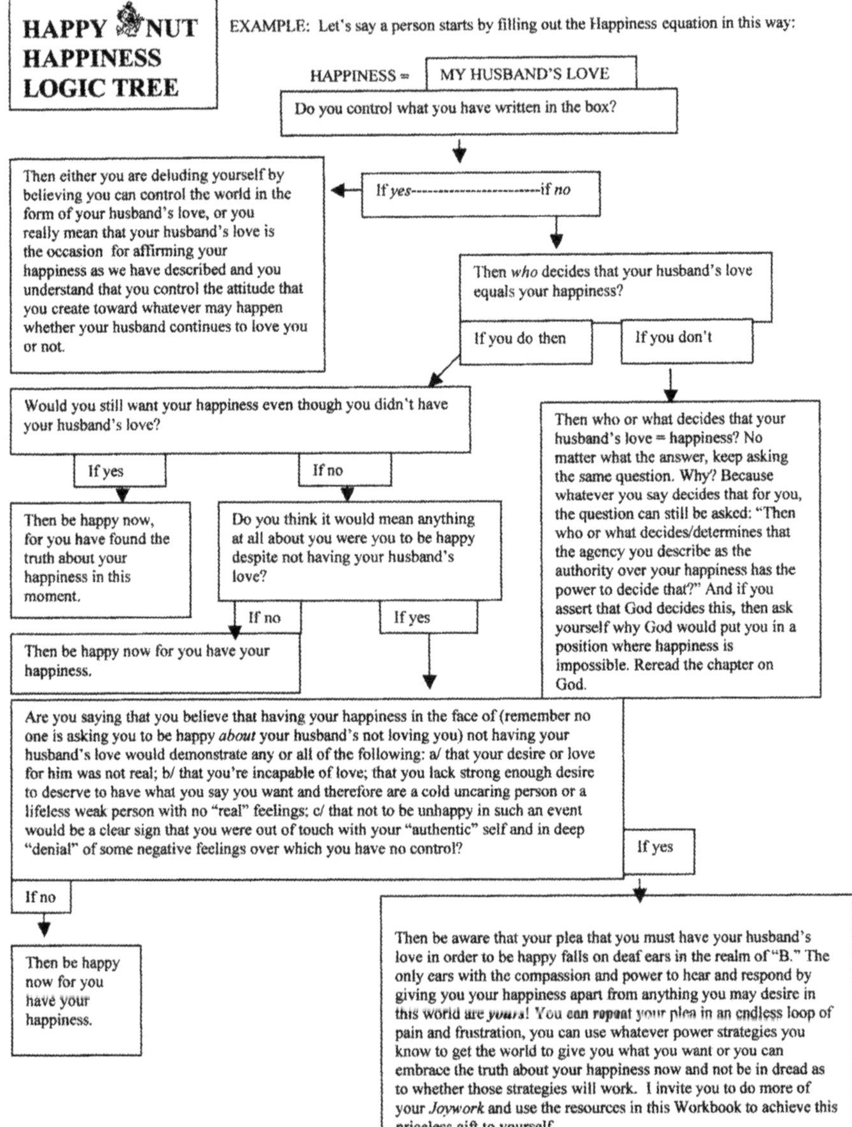
HAPPY NUT HAPPINESS LOGIC TREE
EXAMPLE: Let's say a person starts by filling out the Happiness equation in this way:
HAPPINESS = MY HUSBAND'S LOVE
Do you control what you have written in the box?
If yes----------------------if no
Then either you are deluding yourself by believing you can control the world in the form of your husband's love, or you really mean that your husband's love is the occasion for affirming your happiness as we have described and you understand that you control the attitude that you create toward whatever may happen whether your husband continues to love you or not.
Then who decides that your husband's love equals your happiness?
If you do then
If you don't
Would you still want your happiness even though you didn't have your husband's love?
If yes
If no
Then be happy now, for you have found the truth about your happiness in this moment.
Do you think it would mean anything at all about you were you to be happy despite not having your husband's love?
If no
If yes
Then who or what decides that your husband's love = happiness? No matter what the answer, keep asking the same question. Why? Because whatever you say decides that for you, the question can still be asked: "Then who or what decides/determines that the agency you describe as the authority over your happiness has the power to decide that?" And if you assert that God decides this, then ask yourself why God would put you in a position where happiness is impossible. Reread the chapter on God.
Then be happy now for you have your happiness.
Are you saying that you believe that having your happiness in the face of (remember no one is asking you to be happy about your husband's not loving you) not having your husband's love would demonstrate any or all of the following: a/ that your desire or love for him was not real; b/ that you're incapable of love; that you lack strong enough desire to deserve to have what you say you want and therefore are a cold uncaring person or a lifeless weak person with no "real" feelings; c/ that not to be unhappy in such an event would be a clear sign that you were out of touch with your "authentic" self and in deep "denial" of some negative feelings over which you have no control?
If yes
If no
Then be happy now for you have your happiness.
Then be aware that your plea that you must have your husband's love in order to be happy falls on deaf ears in the realm of "B." The only ears with the compassion and power to hear and respond by giving you your happiness apart from anything you may desire in this world are yours! You can repeat your plea in an endless loop of pain and frustration, you can use whatever power strategies you know to get the world to give you what you want or you can embrace the truth about your happiness now and not be in dread as to whether those strategies will work. I invite you to do more of your Joywork and use the resources in this Workbook to achieve this priceless gift to yourself.

Now let's look at another example where a person sees their happiness as having prosperity, but is troubled by the specter of perhaps not achieving it. Using the Logic Tree may bring some clarification, and further exploration with the Option Method questions can then clear up any remaining issues that arise from the Logic Tree's use.

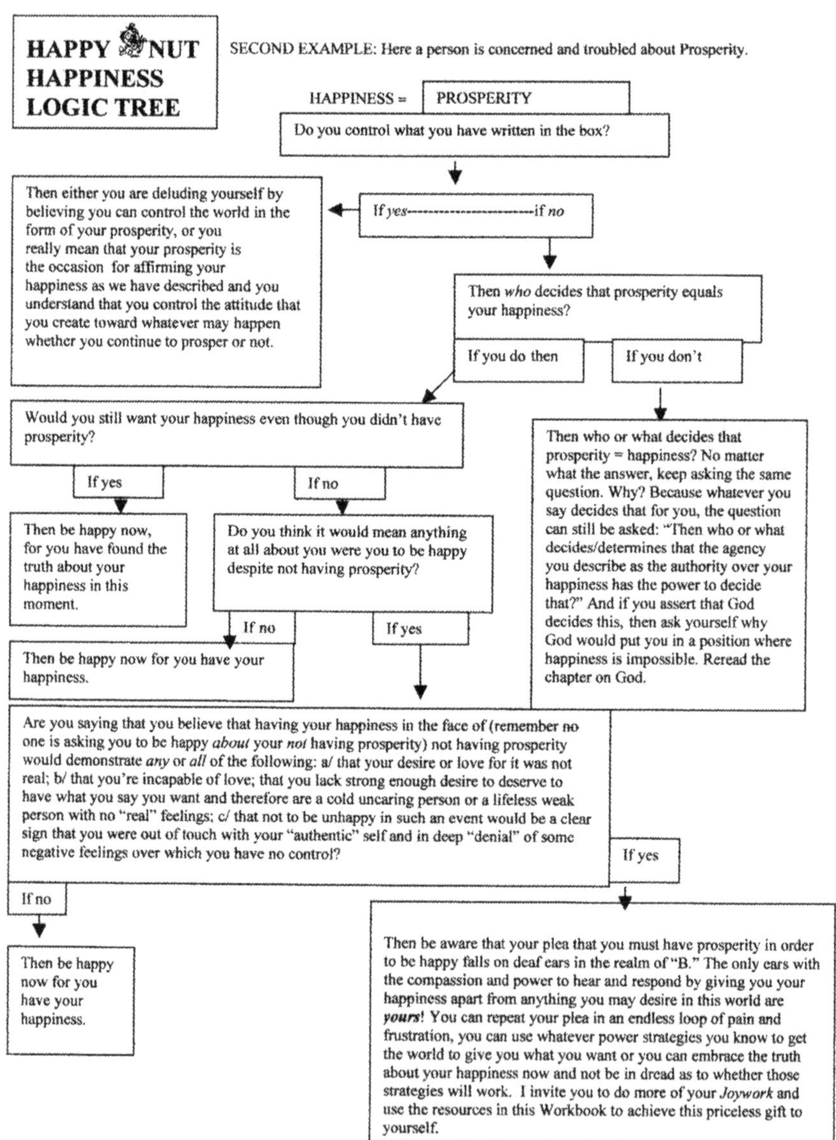
HAPPY NUT
HAPPINESS
LOGIC TREE
SECOND EXAMPLE: Here a person is concerned and troubled about Prosperity.
HAPPINESS = PROSPERITY
Do you control what you have written in the box?
If yes------------------if no
Then either you are deluding yourself by believing you can control the world in the form of your prosperity, or you really mean that your prosperity is the occasion for affirming your happiness as we have described and you understand that you control the attitude that you create toward whatever may happen whether you continue to prosper or not.
Then who decides that prosperity equals your happiness?
If you do then
If you don't
Would you still want your happiness even though you didn't have prosperity?
If yes
If no
Then who or what decides that prosperity = happiness? No matter what the answer, keep asking the same question. Why? Because whatever you say decides that for you, the question can still be asked: "Then who or what decides/determines that the agency you describe as the authority over your happiness has the power to decide that?" And if you assert that God decides this, then ask yourself why God would put you in a position where happiness is impossible. Reread the chapter on God.
Then be happy now, for you have found the truth about your happiness in this moment.
Do you think it would mean anything at all about you were you to be happy despite not having prosperity?
If no
If yes
Then be happy now for you have your happiness.
Are you saying that you believe that having your happiness in the face of (remember no one is asking you to be happy about your not having prosperity) not having prosperity would demonstrate any or all of the following: a/ that your desire or love for it was not real; b/ that you're incapable of love; that you lack strong enough desire to deserve to have what you say you want and therefore are a cold uncaring person or a lifeless weak person with no "real" feelings; c/ that not to be unhappy in such an event would be a clear sign that you were out of touch with your "authentic" self and in deep "denial" of some negative feelings over which you have no control?
If yes
If no
Then be happy now for you have your happiness.
Then be aware that your plea that you must have prosperity in order to be happy falls on deaf ears in the realm of "B." The only ears with the compassion and power to hear and respond by giving you your happiness apart from anything you may desire in this world are yours! You can repeat your plea in an endless loop of pain and frustration, you can use whatever power strategies you know to get the world to give you what you want or you can embrace the truth about your happiness now and not be in dread as to whether those strategies will work. I invite you to do more of your Joywork and use the resources in this Workbook to achieve this priceless gift to yourself.

To give a summary overview again: if you insist that your happiness is the product of your "genes" (nature) or your developmental/cultural circumstances (nurture), then ask yourself if you really believe that you are purely a creature determined only by the influences of the material world and their cultural/socio-political corollaries? If you reply that you are at least partially controlled by the realm of "B" so that some portion of your happiness is not available to you by decisions you make concerning your attitude, then you are still in the same existential dead end. Whatever portion of your equanimity is beyond your control is precisely the part that you dread to encounter and indeed may believe you are experiencing right now. So what you could come to know is that your happiness is always available: you can have it now in your affirmation of it through your freedom (reread my earlier discussions of *Happiness and Time* to orient you in your understanding of what I mean here), or you can remain stuck in the quicksand of the realm of "B." There you will struggle endlessly to reach some "solid ground" of control through the acquisition and use of power, only to find at some point that the ground beneath you will crumble into the shifting terrain of uncertainty and unpredictability. Your power and your castles of control will dissolve and there is nothing you can do about it. That is why all attempts to control the world or any aspect of it fail at some point. No theory or power gained over people or things can be trusted to give the full picture of reality. There will always be some shortcoming or unaccounted for dimension of the world that will ultimately cause a destabilization of whatever structure we knit together out of our cultural, political and personal myths and ideologies. That is where *freedom* enters the picture and you can certainly refresh your memory by referencing what I have said on the subject earlier in this Workbook. Freedom is the correlate of uncertainty in the realm of consciousness, that is to say, all attempts to confine and structure the material world fall short of absolute attainment. Everything is a calculus or approximation of what we perceive the world to be. This is the basis of all technology which creates the wonders of our age but always within the limits of our evolving understanding of how the world works. Freedom represents the utterly unique and incalculable core of what we are; it is the foundational reason why we have our being in the realm of "C" where we can affirm our happiness *now* in the face of whatever the world may present to us out of its mysterious vastness of complexities and unpredictability.

Do you see the wonder of it all? Through our freedom and happiness, we match the unpredictability of the material world with our own ability to create ourselves anew in each moment in the realm of consciousness, of the personal self, of "C." However the world may shift in its vortex of improbabilities as well as its apparently suffocating certainties (death and taxes, etc.), we are ourselves a vast and endless universe of possibilities that no one else can absolutely define or constrain, no matter how certain or hopelessly chaotic life circumstances may seem to be at any given moment. This may be high rhetoric for some, but I hope it will not cloud the direct and simple truth that the universe is rendered a place of hope, meaning and therefore happiness by understanding and accepting the uncompromising truth of our freedom to **be** and to **be** happy whenever we are willing to open our hearts in any given moment and allow that truth to become who we are.

FINAL WORD

Well, Aunt Rose would have been proud that I got the "last word," a tradition that in her case usually was more a sigh than any identifiable language. Truth to say, however, it is you alone that will always have the "last word" with yourself. In some sense, since we are at the mercy of the laws of the world, the realm of "B," every word you utter, coming from whatever belief you may hold and bringing in its wake whatever the corresponding feeling, *may well be your last word!* As you read these lines, it is *now* for you, the only *now* that there is and it continues to be *now* as you read on. You will do with it the very best you know to do. Of that I am absolutely sure. But remember the sharpest knife in the world is the dullest if it is not used. However magnificent the potential of the Option Method may be, if it is not used it will be meaningless. So use it! Employ and apply what you have learned. Why not? You have already worked hard to have your joy. Now reap the rewards of continuing to feel happier and even happier still. I do invite you, indeed this whole Joybuilding enterprise has been an invitation to your happiness. This Method is not some religious dogma. But, I suppose, for some it can be made into a straitjacket and experienced as a burden if one is disposed to do so. Of course that has nothing to do with my intention for you or with the true and genuinely liberating message that it represents for me as I write these words.

So, I urge you to wear this Method lightly; let it be like your skin, a totally natural garment that you notice only as an instrument for sensuous loving exploration with yourself and others. I leave you with words left to me by my mentor. May they be what you affirm for yourself now even as you read them and hold them in the bosom of your awareness for each *now* that you are privileged to experience:

All people are allowed to be happy at all times, forever. This is happiness; to know you are always allowed to be happy no matter who you are, what you do and no matter what happens to you.
To be blessed is to have the right to be happy. To be born is to be allowed to be happy. To know you are allowed to be happy is to be blessed.
It is evident. God permits you to be happy no matter what or when Nature permits you to be happy no matter what or when. The only permission you need is yours to be happy all the time.
You don't ever have to deny your happiness ever. It is not wrong to be happy always. Bruce M. DiMarsico

About the Author

Frank Mosca Ph.D. is an Option Educator and motivational expert with a private practice in Hampton Bays, N.Y. He has a background in the Humanities as a former Professor at N.Y. University, and in Psychology, having received Graduate and Post Graduate training at the N.Y. University Post Doctoral Institute for Psychotherapy and at other institutions. He has published on topics as varied as hypnosis, altered states, and chaos theory. After years of training with Bruce Di Marsico the founder of the Option Method, Frank now lectures locally and nationally. Additional works include *Joywords, The Unbearable Wrongness of Being*, a novel, *The God Speak*, audio tapes and constant updates and timely topics that can be found on his website *http://frankmosca.com* . He can be contacted by e-mail at *frank@frankmosca.com* or by phone at 631-728-5912.

0-595-21774-5

Lightning Source UK Ltd.
Milton Keynes UK
UKHW012237011021
391519UK00001B/158